The Life of a River

The Life of a River

ANDY RUSSELL

A DOUGLAS GIBSON BOOK

M&S

McClelland & Stewart trade paperback edition published 2000
First published in hardcover by McClelland & Stewart 1987

Canadian Cataloguing in Publication Data

Russell, Andy, 1915–
    The life of a river

ISBN 0-7710-7878-1 (bound)   ISBN 0-7710-7876-5 (pbk.)

1. Oldman River Valley (Alta.) – History.   I. Title.

QH106.2.A4R88 2000   971.23'4   C87-094624-2

We acknowledge the financial support of the Government of Canada through
the Book Publishing Industry Development Program for our publishing
activities. We further acknowledge the support of the Canada Council for the
Arts and the Ontario Arts Council for our publishing program.

Printed and bound in Canada

A Douglas Gibson Book

McClelland & Stewart Inc.
The Canadian Publishers
481 University Avenue
Toronto, Ontario
M5G 2E9

1 2 3 4 5   04 03 02 01 00

to Zahava

Contents

Prologue

The Way Things Were

The man sat with his back to a clump of stunted birch high up near the brow of a ridge among the Porcupine Hills in what is now Alberta. His eyes missed nothing that moved across the vast stretch of brush- and grass-covered country below him. A herd of horses suddenly galloped into view pursued by a pack of wolves, but he gave them only a fleeting glance as they ran past a hundred Athabascan bison feeding on a bluff. The man had his eyes on a partially hidden hollow at the bottom of a sloping basin half a mile below and to one side of him. Birch and aspen grew thick there and every few minutes one or two of the trees waved and jerked, giving away something big feeding out of his sight.

The brush suddenly began to ripple and sway in a line pointing to the near edge of the hollow. Suddenly a big bull hairy mammoth broke into view, the ivory of his great twelve-foot tusks framing his head and trunk in a gleaming curved outline that contrasted sharply with the dark-brown hair and wool covering his entire body. He was a sight to make any hunter's heart pick up a beat.

Right behind him came an old cow, not as large, but massive just the same. The big bones of her hips and shoulders showed through the new growth of her coat, which still included the old

bleached-out patches of unshed hair and wool here and there that
spoke of her years and of a long, tough preceding winter. At her
heels came a first-year calf. Then one by one came a line of twenty-
odd mammoths of various sizes and ages, young bulls and cows, two
or three more mature cows with calves, and, a bit behind the string,
another big bull. At a steady walk they filed up a grassy slope at a
long angle and finally swung directly toward the watching man,
whose eyes were fastened on the last bull. They came over a saddle
on the near side of a ridge and slanted down another slope to the
edge of a steep-sided gully, where a whitewater creek ran down
toward the river.

There the lead bull stopped, as though contemplating the way
down the steeply pitched bank of gravel and loose rock. Swinging
his trunk and rocking his tusks, he sidestepped down off the edge
and went ploughing toward the stream at an angle. Every animal
followed him, and by the time the last of the line came to the top,
the herd's feet had crushed the gravel into a smooth pathway. The
last bull paused at the top of the bank, watching the rest of the big
animals lining up shoulder to shoulder for a drink, before following
to take his position lower down.

He was a young animal, though fully grown, his new coat deep
brown and his tusks massive, though not as big as those of the lead
bull. On one flank the man's keen eyes could see a long scar almost
grown over with wool and hair, a severe brand that the older bull
had no doubt inflicted for his brashness in challenging him for the
favours of a cow in heat earlier in the summer. A painful wound, it
did nothing to improve his temper, which, the man knew, was
none too sweet at the best of times.

Almost directly above them now, the man stood up, slung the
carrying-strap of his pouch across his shoulders, and picked up a
matched trio of spears and his throwing-stick. Leaning on the spear
shafts, he continued to watch. Like all good hunters, he was a man
of great patience. Lean, well-muscled, and powerful, his every line
was as wild and free as the peregrine falcon perched on the tip of the

rocky point behind him, lit up in the early-morning sun. His name was Big Tooth. The time was summer, 30,000 years before the present.

Big Tooth knew every animal in this herd very well, for he had been watching them for days, studying their feeding patterns, and testing their reaction to the sight and smell of him, sometimes at very close range. They had become so accustomed to his presence that they scarcely paid any attention any more – all but the young bull wearing the scar, who showed fight every time he saw the hunter. Once the bull had almost caught him, when in escaping from a charge he failed to see a boggy spot in time and landed in it up to his knees. Big Tooth bared his teeth in a wolfish grin as he remembered the narrow escape. There was a score to settle and a dream to complete, a dream that had told him that he and this scarred bull were destined to fight to the death.

Four summers before, when he had been a stripling keen to join the hunters of his band, the medicine man had sent him off alone, as was the way of his people when the time came for a young man to seek his naming dream. He had climbed up to a big tree growing on a ledge on a cliff many miles from here, close to the ice, where peaks sticking up from it overlooked a lake in the corridor further north, a favourite spot for the big white-headed eagles to nest. Following the medicine man's directions, he had nothing to eat or drink, carried only his spear, and wore nothing but his breech-clout. If the spirits so willed, they would bring him water, but he could not move away from the tree in search of it.

He had never known time to move so slowly. During the day, when it was baking hot, with little shade, he stood or sat with his back to the tree, watching its shadow swing as the sun moved slow-ly across the sky. He saw a pair of eagles fly out from their nest atop another tree farther up the cliff, as they swung and climbed on the thermals hunting for food for their young. They were the friends of old Eagle Speaker, the medicine man, and told him many things:

the best herb roots and leaves for healing wounds and curing belly-aches and fever. The boy watched one of the eagles stoop like a fall-ing spear out of the clouds and kill a marmot in a patch of boulders and carry it up to the nest. He eyed the marmot hungrily, his stomach growling, and worked out a route to climb up and steal what was left of it, but then put the thought resolutely from his mind. At night he curled up in a kind of nest he had made from green twigs broken from the tree and a little grass he had gathered from around its base. It was cold there when the sun went down, with the smell of glacier ice on the night air. Fortunately the nights were short at that time of year.

On the third morning he watched the sun come up hotter than ever, wondering if the spirits meant him to die here without giving him a dream. Then a black cloud shot through with lightning bolts blotted out the sun, the thunder came with deafening explosions, and the lightning struck the top of the cliff over his head, along with rain that fell in great sheets. The boy caught it in his cupped hands and sucked it up, feeling it spread deliciously through his parched body. Then a great blinding shaft of lightning shivered atop the eagles' nesting-tree, followed by an ear-splitting crack. When his eyes came back into focus, the nest was gone; the tree smoked and steamed with a new white scar showing from its top to its roots. The sun came out again, warm and lovely, soothing away his shivering as he watched the towering cloud of the storm moving up the valley, the lightning still dancing to the rolling of its reced-ing thunder drums.

That night the air was uncommonly balmy and the boy slept deeply for the first time under a brilliant canopy of stars in a cloud-less sky. Suddenly it was there facing him, so close he could smell its fetid breath – a great mammoth bull with tusks red with blood and eyes that glowed like coals fresh from the campfire. It towered over him, blotting out the sky and trapping him against the cliff. He reached for his spear, to find it grown so big that he could scarcely lift it, then swung it around with its tip pointing at the bull, its butt against the solid rock. The monster spread its great ears, blew a blast of rank-smelling air at him, rolled up its trunk between its eyes, and came at him. The stone spear point glanced off the base of a tusk, skidded through the wool of its shoulder, and opened a bloody gash along its flank. Then the spear broke off and the bull screamed, rearing high over him – to suddenly fall backward off the cliff. The boy woke to his own scream, his eyes blinded by the rising sun and his body drenched with sweat.

On shaking legs he climbed down off the cliff to the forest and the trail that would lead him to camp. When he arrived there, the people all greeted him as he tried to walk proud and tall, drawing on his innermost strength to keep from tottering.

Eagle Speaker came to him, his fierce old eyes reading him at a glance, and taking him by the arm he led him across to the fire, where they both sat down, sharing the same skin. Reaching into his pouch, the old man mixed various things in a hollowed-out rock, which he proceeded to grind up with another stone. Taking a horn ladle, he next dipped some soup from the trough by the fire and mixed the concoction into it by stirring with a stick. Handing it to the youngster, he bade him drink it. The taste was sharp, but not unpleasant, and the feel of it spread like a glow until it seemed to make his very fingers and toes tingle. He looked longingly at the meat in the trough, but Eagle Speaker took the ladle back and shook his head. So for a while the boy just sat there enjoying the warmth of the potion till his eyes became heavy and he could no longer keep them open. Then he rolled over on his side and slept.

When he woke up, it was sunset. He felt enormously refreshed and utterly ravenous. His mother, Shining Star, a strong woman with a purposeful way about her and a wide smile, handed him a slab of bark piled with steaming meat, which he proceeded to eat like a hungry wolf. Then he helped himself to some more. His father, Bear Paw, the chief of this band, came and invited him to join the council at his dome-shaped wickiup of hides supported by mammoth ribs. The council formed a ring around a fire built in front of it and the people circled them.

Eagle Speaker took his place by the chief, then rose and extracted from his pouch certain herbs and grass, which he burnt on the fire. Holding his hands to the smoke, he went to Bear Paw and rubbed his fingertips on his forehead, before doing the same for every member of the council. After a considerable pause, during which there was no sound except the crackling of the fire, Bear Paw rose to his feet and made a short speech.

Reaching down, he took the boy by the arm and said, "You have been on the first hunt. Tell us about it." Then he sat down.

At first the boy was hesitant, but then he recalled how other hunters told their stories around evening fires, and he warmed up and his voice expressed excitement. When he told about the storm and how the lightning bolt came down to wipe out the eagles' nest and blast the bark from the tree, there was a ripple of exclamations around the fire and some of the council covered their mouths with their hands, the sign of great astonishment. After a pause, the boy told of his dream, not losing anything in the telling, as the vivid recollection of his dream animated his voice and made his eyes shine. Suddenly conscious of being carried away by his own story, he sat down, his head bowed, looking at his feet.

Old Eagle Speaker stood up again, quiet for a while, then he reached down into that marvellous pouch of his and took out a small leather bag dark with grease, untied the top of it, and signalled the boy to rise to his feet. Holding the bag aloft, he intoned a powerful prayer calling on all the spirits of the sky and earth to witness this great medicine and to give the boy all the power and protection needed by a mighty hunter. Finally, dipping his fingers into the bag he proceeded with deft art to draw a jagged line in red paint across the boy's forehead depicting the lightning, then the sign of the sun on either cheek, strength signs on his shoulders, and other equally significant symbols on his back and legs. On the chest he drew a very fair sketch of a mammoth bull coming head-on with outstretched ears and great tusks.

Then, placing both hands on top of the boy's head, he said, "You have met the spirits. You are now a man. I give you the name of Big Tooth."

That had been four summers ago, and now Big Tooth was in the prime of manhood. He was taller than most of his peers, his finely muscled body wide in the shoulders and narrow at the hips, with a deep chest from running across this rugged land, sometimes for hours without a break. He was an experienced hunter, recognized as a leader. He was a scout who ranged alone much of the time keeping track of the herds of animals sharing this territory with his band, as well as a messenger between his people and others scattered across this country which would one day be drained by the Oldman River.

Now he watched as the mammoths crossed the stream to climb the opposite bank up onto a bench, where they proceeded to bunch up in the sun to digest their morning's feed. He set off down the slope at a long, striding walk toward the massive animals. They paid him no attention, for as usual he wove an indirect pattern of approach, never looking at them directly for more than a moment, pausing here and there, and giving the impression that they were of no interest to him.

As he came up to them, the big bull with the scar was on the far side of the herd, the herd bull was in the middle of the group, and nearest him were some cows. The hunter circled with casual motions that were smooth as silk, and when he passed within a few steps of a dry cow, she flapped her ears and blew at him but did not move her feet. As he expected, the scarred one was slightly separated from the herd, so he circled wide to come to a stop directly in front of the animal about fifty steps away. For a while they eyed each other without moving; then the bull raised his trunk and blew angrily. Big Tooth set about deliberately taunting him by dancing forward and back. The huge animal spread its ears and glared. Then suddenly it charged in a deceptively fast rush. Big Tooth stood poised, absolutely still till the last moment, before leaping to the side, allowing the bull's momentum to carry him past. Without losing a step he shot across behind the bull, giving him a solid blow across the flat of his rump with the shafts of his spears. When the bull swung around, Big Tooth was gone, hidden in a clump of brush. The bull charged back toward the herd, stopped, and turned to see the hated two-legged one once more taunting him on the edge of the drop-off toward the creek. His eyes red and bulging with rage, the bull charged again with a speed and agility amazing for such sheer bulk.

Again, just a split second ahead of utter destruction, the hunter dodged aside and the bull's speed carried him over the edge, to go skidding down with a great clatter of stones toward the water. This time Big Tooth followed him closely, stabbing his victim several times on his exposed rear, until the monster found some traction at the bottom and swung around screaming with fury. As usual, his tormentor was gone. Several of the herd had come to stand on the rim, no doubt trying to figure out what was causing the uproar.

Then Big Tooth appeared again, running easily on a slant up the far side of the gully back along the mammoths' trail. At the top of the saddle he looked back and saw the bull climbing back up toward the bench, and his teeth gleamed again. This one was ready. There was a fine line to be drawn in this game, and he knew that overdoing the taunting would go against his plans, for the bull would learn the folly of blind rushes and become very difficult, if not impossible, to handle.

The morning was still young as he set out at a long trot for camp several miles up a river. The sun was still only halfway to its zenith overhead when he walked into the camp of his people, and headed for the fire smouldering in front of his father's wickiup, where the chief was sitting talking to old Eagle Speaker. As he approached, Eagle Speaker's sharp, deep-set brown eyes studied him from under a headband of fur decorated with little bones that rattled when he moved.

"I have seen him," Big Tooth told them. "The bull with the scar on his flank – the one of my dream."

His father covered his mouth with his hand, his eyes widening with surprise. Eagle Speaker grunted, as though confirming that this was not news to him.

"I have been with him and his herd for seven suns," Big Tooth told them. "He is ready. I am going to kill him. It is my dream."

Again Eagle Speaker grunted and his father said, "When the sun goes behind the mountains we will talk."

Big Tooth leaned his spear against the side of the wickiup, set down his pouch, and turned to the fire, where he ladled a chunk of elk meat out of the steaming trough heated by hot rocks. He squatted on his heels, his eyes roving around the camp as he ate ravenously.

Between him and the river he saw Sun Gazer, the band's flint-knapper, his squat, powerful body straddling a log as he studied a rock in front of him. At long intervals, he turned the rock a bit and studied it from a different angle. Standing back to one side, leaning on their spears, a small group of hunters stood patiently waiting. After demolishing another chunk of meat, Big Tooth wiped his hand across his mouth, tossed away a bone, and walked over to join them. They greeted him quietly, careful not to disturb the concentration of the man on the log.

It was not till the sun was directly overhead that Sun Gazer picked up the stone in both hands to lift it high and slowly turn it in final examination of its every minute detail. Then he set it down again on the log directly in front of him. Picking up the specially shaped striking-stone that fitted the palm of his big hand, he lifted it and brought it down sharply but with the utmost precision on top of the rock at its edge. Like magic, a long, flat sliver of flint fell away. Slightly turning the stone each time, he struck it with exactly the same rhythm and tempo again and again, and just as often a flake of the flint was knocked free. By the time he had turned it a full 360 degrees, the stone was the shape of an inverted cone sitting on its small end, perfectly balanced.

For a few minutes he studied it. Then, with a grunt of satisfaction, he struck it again, and a long, perfectly tapered flake dropped, which he picked up and set to one side. Again and again the striking stone came down, shearing off flakes, until all that was left of the original rock was a circular-shaped tapered core. Picking up the flakes, he held them up and examined them one by one against the sun. They were opaque – almost clear toward the edges in places. Only one of them showed a flaw and was discarded.

Picking up a curiously shaped tool made of deer horn, he proceeded to work on one of the flakes. Sometimes tapping the horn into gripping the flint, sometimes aided by gentle taps of the hammer, he deftly twisted off tiny flakes, quickly shaping the long, double-edged point of a spear. He flattened it at the base, chipped two notches on each side of it to hold the binding thongs, and carefully smoothed these so they would not cut the rawhide. Then he worked in the distinctive groove running from the base up the blade a third of its length which would accommodate the shaped shaft tip. Finally he proceeded to smooth the edges, drawing them down to a fine point. When he was finished it was much more than just a utilitarian spear point – it was a beautifully crafted object of real art, a Clovis point as it would become known.

Sun Gazer then passed the point to a waiting hunter and began to work on another.

Big Tooth slipped away up the slope back of the camp where there was a projecting sandstone ledge. Reaching under it, he drew forth a long pole, all of three times as long and heavy as a throwing-spear, which had been cut from a carefully selected green birch with only a few small knots. It had been scraped, smoothed, straightened, and cured slowly where the sun never shone on it. He had kept the making of it secret.

Carrying it out, he rejoined the group still standing near Sun Gazer, balanced it on end, and waited. The length of the shaft brought some grunts of astonishment from several of the hunters, but the artist on the log paid no attention. Finally, when the time came, he looked inquiringly at Big Tooth, who pointed to the circular core of the flint stone that had been left when the flakes had been chipped away. Lowering the long shaft, he indicated how he wanted it fitted to the already shaped tip. Sun Gazer examined it, turning the stone first one way and then the other before beginning to chip away at it, drawing the taper of the flint core down to a sharp point. His fingers flew and the thing seemed to grow in his hands almost as though it was soft instead of being among the hardest stones found on earth. Finally, he shaped the base carefully, keeping it square to the centre line of the rounded point. When he was satisfied, he handed it to Big Tooth, who grinned when he held it against the socketed tip of the longest, heaviest lance any hunter had ever seen.

He took the shaft and point down to the spring, where some rawhide thongs were tied under water to a submerged willow root. Being wet, the thongs were pliable and easily stretched to fit the contours of the point and shaft tip. Selecting a long thong and a shorter and wider piece, he carried the components for his mighty weapon down the stream to a long, low bank and sat down. Behind him several of the women were working with skins, but beyond a curious glance or two they paid him scant attention.

Using a pointed flint knife with a marvellously keen edge, Big Tooth cut a hole in the middle of the wider piece of rawhide, slipped it over the point, and snugged it down around the base over the socket. Trimming the hanging ends so they would sandwich the shaft with no overlap, he then cut small holes along the edges. He took a piece of thong, stretched it carefully till it was thin, and stitched the rawhide around the wood, forming a snug sleeve. He wound the rest of the thong around the base of the point, pulling it up hard at every turn as he wove it on down the shaft twice the width of his hand, where he tied it off. Then, with the remaining length of rawhide, he started at the top again and repeated the process, taking it even farther down the shaft. When that was done, he leaned the spear up against a tall sapling growing near by to dry the rawhide in the sun, before he rubbed some grease into it. The drying would shrink it and set it as hard as the wood.

That evening there was excitement at the sunset, for the word had got around that Big Tooth had made an enormous spear. When the council gathered, Eagle Speaker proceeded with the usual opening smoke ritual. Bear Paw stood up and paused for a long time, silently looking at the sky. Then he asked his son to speak.

So Big Tooth told them what he had been doing for seven suns. He told them about the bad-tempered bull mammoth and how he had watched and prepared him. "He is the one of my dream – he wears the scar. Tomorrow I will go with five hunters. It would please me, O Chief, if you would pick them. When we come to the long-nosed ones, I will fight him and kill him – alone. No one will throw a spear unless he kills me. Then the hunters can let his blood run out on the ground."

"He will kill you," snarled one of the hunters, a tall man standing back of the council ring. "He will kill you," he repeated. "No hunter has ever killed a long-nosed one alone!"

The tall hunter, who had a terrible scar on his face from a fight with an enraged bear, then shook his head and said nothing more.

For a while the council sat unmoving, then one by one they placed their hands palm-down on the tops of their heads, signifying that they granted their permission. The hunters were chosen, among them the fierce-looking Scarface. That night there was no story-telling, no drums or dancing. Everyone went to their sleeping-skins quietly, for this was an unheard-of thing. As he flattened out his bed of soft tanned furs, Scarface shook his head again, for Big Tooth was the one who had saved him from the bear. He knew that if it hadn't been for the dream, the council might have stopped this foolishness.

At dawn the whole camp was stirring with preparations for the hunt. The hunters would go ahead, but every person in camp able to travel would follow, not just to see the fight, if possible, but to carry back meat.

The hunters took three spears apiece and their spear-throwers. Big Tooth carried only the long one. Dressed in moccasins and breech-clouts, their hair tied back at the nape of the neck with a cord, they left camp at a fast walk heading for high ground before turning downriver following the slope. Big Tooth was in the lead and he chose a way along a high bench overlooking the country below. By mid-morning they were on a rocky point not far from where he had last seen the mammoths. There was no sign of them, so the hunters strung out, heading for a jutting shoulder ahead. Again there was nothing to be seen of the quarry, so they moved on. This time they had not gone far when Big Tooth stopped and pointed with his spear. Down in a grassy basin surrounded on three sides by brushy slopes, the mammoths were taking their morning rest after filling their bellies with feed.

Big Tooth led the hunters down the slope. When they came to the rim of an open shelf just over the floor of the basin, he motioned to the others to wait there and then went down toward the huge beasts to scout casually along the open edge of the meadow. The herd were about one hundred and fifty steps away, all lazing in the sun flapping their ears on occasion. As usual, the bull wearing the scar was separated a bit to one side. If he was to have a fair chance of making the kill, Big Tooth had not only to lure the bull away from the herd, but also to pick a spot to meet it with the spear.

In front of him a shallow channel made by spring meltwater, but now dry, swung in a curve; it was rimmed by a low bank with a gently sloping gravel bar opposite. Big Tooth looked it over and found it just what he wanted. He crossed the dry wash and laid his spear flat on the gravel with its stone tip pointing at the bull.

Then, as casually as he would stroll into camp, he walked toward the bull, which was standing with its tail squarely to him, swaying gently on its feet, apparently sound asleep. If any of the rest of the

herd saw him, they paid no attention, and Big Tooth finally came
to a stop barely twenty steps from the sleeping bull. For a few
moments he stood motionless, then turned to check the spear before
letting his eyes swing up onto the ridge. Up above, some of the
people were already lined up watching, and others were filing into
view. Turning again, he looked around him, and spotting an arm-
length stick as thick as his wrist he stepped sideways to pick it up.
Winding up, he flung it hard and caught the bull squarely across
the root of the tail.

For a moment the bull never moved, then the great animal
turned broadside and froze. With seeming casualness Big Tooth
turned his back toward it, bent over, and flipped the rear flap of his
breech-clout up and down. The bull blew an angry blast as it came
around to face him, then spread its ears and raised its trunk. But it
froze again, seeming to doubt what it saw. The hunter danced backward toward it, still flapping the breech-clout, while he watched
over his shoulder. When he had gone three or four steps, the bull
suddenly blew another great trumpeting blast and Big Tooth leapt
away as it charged.

The hunter dug in his toes and sprinted straight for his waiting
spear, gaining a little ground, then holding it. When he reached
the spear, he came to a sliding halt, grasped the middle of the shaft,
and slid the butt back against the bank. Centring the point, he
barely had time to aim it low under the bull's jaw for the hollow at
the base of the neck, just over the brisket bone. At the impact, Big
Tooth braced himself, with all his weight on the upward straining
bow of the tough, seasoned shaft. The spear went deep into the
bull's chest – deeper than he had expected, for he was almost under
that mighty trunk and the sharp tusks curled over his head. Then
the spear shaft broke and he leapt sideways just in time to miss
being wiped out by the clubbing trunk. The bull pivoted toward
him, blowing a great blast of air and blood that turned Big Tooth
crimson from head to foot, momentarily blinding him. With the
broken shaft standing out from its chest, the bull followed him. As

the hunter dodged, pawing blood out of his eyes, he slipped on the gravel and went down. Rolling sideways, he barely missed being trampled under the raging animal's great feet, but he recovered in time to regain his footing and grab the bull's tail. The mammoth swung in a full circle, screaming and bellowing, showering blood in every direction, with the man joining in with a war-cry of his own as he clung grimly to the tail, off the ground more than he was on it.

Then the rest of the herd arrived, and Big Tooth found himself surrounded by the great, blood-crazed beasts, their feet thundering and tusks clashing as they trumpeted and milled around in confusion. Spotting an opening, he let go and dashed for the brush, only to have a half-grown cow almost run him down. He grabbed a double handful of its long hair and vaulted up onto its back, whereupon it squealed like a great pig and spun in its own length, but he had a good grip and stuck like a burr. The cow carried him clear around the milling herd with the stricken bull in its middle, and when it came through a tongue of brush, he leapt off, to instantly disappear.

When Big Tooth had climbed through the brush high enough to be clear and able to see, the bull was down on its hindquarters, sitting propped up by its forelegs, its breath coming with great heaves. The ground was red with blood and it showed copiously on the flanks of the animals still milling around him and shattering the clear mountain air with their trumpeting. Suddenly the mighty animal lifted its head high, pointing its trunk and tusks at the sky; then it sagged, rolling over on its side to lie still.

Scarface arrived through the brush to grasp the hunter's shoulder, his face twisted in a lopsided grin. Then the other four hunters came on the run to join him, their eyes blazing with excitement. Their blood was up, and it was obvious that they wanted to try for another kill. But Big Tooth shook his head. "Enough," he said. "The spirit of all hunters says no more this sun." And they complied, for he was the chosen leader of this hunt, though they showed their disappointment.

The rest of the people began to arrive, chattering and exclaiming; Sun Gazer, Bear Paw, and even old grey-haired Eagle Speaker placed their hands on his shoulders in the age-old tribute of one hunter to another.

Their frenzy spent, the mammoths suddenly stopped their wild milling and tore away at a gallop, leaving the scarred bull, ten thousand pounds of dead meat, bone, and hide, behind them. Big Tooth led the way to the huge carcass. Reaching down to grasp the stub of the spear protruding from the chest, with difficulty he tugged it clear. It had penetrated almost a third of its length, and the stone tip was broken.

Now the butchering began. Using their razor-sharp flint knives, some with the blades lashed in a cleft stick, others held in the hand, the people took that huge carcass apart with amazing speed. By the time the sun was halfway down to the western horizon, all that was left was the big bones, the tusks, and a huge pile of offal surrounded by heaps of red meat. As a long line of people strung out carrying big loads, smoky green-wood fires were lit all around the spot to keep off scavengers till all the meat could be relayed into camp, where it would be cut up and dried.

Back at camp it was a time of celebration, of feasting and joyful dancing in homage to the successful hunter. The full moon lit up the council circle around the fire in front of Bear Paw's lodge, where the trough was full of rich soup, seasoned with herbs, and boiled meat. The stars of the Big Bear swung and the eastern horizon was lightening when Bear Paw rose to his feet, lifting his hands for silence.

"My son," he said. "You have made a dream live for all of us. You have shown us a new way to kill the long-nosed ones. It is for you to have a gift from us — any gift you ask for. Choose now!"

Big Tooth stood up. "O Chief, I am grateful. I will choose!"

His eyes roved around the circle and then fastened on the slim form of a girl standing just on the edge of the firelight. Walking over, he took her by the arm and led her away to his sleeping-skins, while the people returned to their singing and dancing.

So it was on a summer night 30,000 years ago in the Porcupine Hills, when the people celebrated the first single-handed killing of a giant hairy mammoth.

Pure fiction, you say? Maybe – but also maybe not. You will have a very rough time proving it, while I will smile, for I know that this part of the world, south of Calgary and just east of the Rockies and the foothills, never iced up until very late in the time of the glaciers, and I have seen unmistakable evidence that mammoths and many other animals ranged here and were hunted by the people of that period. From up high on the mountains, I have sat alone under the shimmering, hissing curtains of the aurora borealis and communed with the spirits of the people who were here ages ago – the early descendants of those enterprising ones who came across from Asia on the land-bridge into Alaska. They left indelible tracks in the form of their stone tools and the knife-scarred bones and ivory still preserved in the middens of their old camps. And, as you will hear, at a dig near Taber, Alberta, archaeologists have found a skeleton fully 40,000 years old.

So before you get too set in your opinion, listen for a while to an old modern-day hunter, who knows what it is to eat and feed his family with the meat taken with his weapons. He has only been in spirit with those old Clovis people who populated and hunted in what is now southern Alberta as early as 40,000 or more years ago. We haven't found all the tracks yet by any means, but we have found enough to outline a picture – a fascinating part of the history of North America.

But first you have to be able to look at a river and see something more than water sliding down from the top of the Continental Divide to its juncture with the sea. For those with eyes to see, a river can be a living link with our past.

Introduction

When most of us look at a river, we do not pause to consider the many chapters of its history. We rarely pause to ponder its close ties with various human cultures; not only with the people who have lived along its banks, but also with those who have evolved with it and even preceded it, while the land was being formed.

I remember my grandfather and my father telling of building their houses on the old ranch in southern Alberta at the confluence of Pothole Creek and the St. Mary's River, a few miles southwest of what is now the city of Lethbridge. My grandfather was one of the earliest white settlers in this part of the West, arriving in 1882. The history of European influence in Alberta spans only about two hundred and twenty-five years, and it was only about a hundred years ago that this impact involved agriculture; for the grazing of cattle on the open range preceded the homesteading era when the sod began to be turned under to grow cereal grains. My father, the first white baby born in the Lethbridge area, was nearly twenty years old when Alberta officially became a province of the Dominion of Canada in 1905. When he got married, he proceeded to build a home not far from my grandfather's house, and, like him, he built it out of concrete made from the natural limestone found on the surrounding land.

First he dug a pit near the edge of a perpendicular clay bank overlooking the river close by. This hole was about four feet across by twenty feet deep – hard spadework, as you can imagine – and when he got down to bedrock just over a seam of coal exposed by the river, he dug a lateral drift in to meet it. This he shaped into a firebox lined with field stone overlaid on top with a heavy grate made of steel rails from an abandoned railway spur. He also lined the clay sides above the grate with carefully fitted rock, just as the hand-dug water wells of that time were shored up to keep them from caving in. He then filled the hole with loose chunks of pure limestone. At this point, using the natural coal seam, he set a hot fire under it, the draft carrying the heat up through the lime as in a chimney. Keeping the fire going day and night, he thus fired the lime to make his cement, which he poured into forms to construct the outside walls of the new house – a house that still stands solidly eighty years later, a monument to the man who built it for shelter for his new bride.

But I doubt if even he, though he was a very observant and questioning man, realized the historical significance of what he had done, for generally a man involved in such hard manual labour does not have the time to pause and ponder even things that are staring him squarely in the eye. Everything involved with the use of that lime – the limestone itself, the clay he had dug through to make his kiln, and the coal he had fired it with – represented pages of history covering eons of time.

The story went back many millions of years to the days when this land was covered by an ocean, and when hordes of minute shellfish on the ocean bottom laid down the sediment that was the making of the limestone. Later, when the waters of this great sea receded, they were replaced by steaming jungles growing in quaking swamps; the exotic plants that grew there in their turn built up great beds of

dead vegetation that formed the coal seams. Then came the ice ages
to pulverize the rock of the earth's crust, adding to and creating the
fine silt forming the overburden of clay. When the climate warmed
again, great lakes of meltwater from the ice were formed. And this
water gradually made trickles that formed streams, which built into
rivers like the St. Mary, which in turn flowed into other rivers to
become the mighty Saskatchewan rolling east and north until eventually it ran into Hudson Bay.

It was thus our river system was born, including the St. Mary,
which as a very small boy I could look across from our window to
the ice-contoured slopes of the hills and draws across the valley. We
shared those hills covered with rich buffalo grass with the Blood Indians, a recently tamed tribe of the great Blackfoot Nation that had
fiercely resisted the intrusion of the white man, but in vain. Our
cattle and horses grazed along with theirs; cattle that had taken the
place of the hordes of buffalo, and horses descended from those
brought by the early Spanish conquistadors. History has a way of
losing itself in time, then jumping swiftly into a new era. We were
a part of that fast transition when the buffalo, elk, antelope, and
other wildlife had been deposed by us, with the Indians relegated to
the confines of reservations. Even the rivers were first deflected into
ditches to grow gardens and hay and later dammed and used for
more irrigation and energy.

This book, I hope, will make us look again at the conventional
wisdom of using a river as a resource, not treating it as a living
thing. For as nature builds a river, it is a celebration of life, and a
happy and continuing promise of life. A river is wild and thus
something of a mystery. It can be violent and dangerous, or serene
and very lovely, icy cold or sensuously warm. Wherever it runs on
its inevitable journey to the sea, it is a kind of magnet drawing
lesser streams within its watershed to it as well as all forms of life.

A river does not just happen; it has a beginning and an end. Its
story is written in rich earth, in ice, and in water-carved stone, and

its story as the lifeblood of the land is filled with colour, music, and thunder.

A river is only local to those who do not think or have not learned to see. It can be tamed, but it resents it. And then far-reaching and very destructive things happen, all the way from the trickles of its source clear down to its deltas and estuaries at the edge of the ocean, and even out into the salt water.

As an example, this is the story of the river I know best, the Oldman River in what is now southern Alberta. It is a story that can be transposed to any river – and to the animals, birds, fish, and men who have lived and are now living along its banks – all beginning many thousands of years ago.

1 *In the Very Beginning*

Nobody knows for sure how it happened. Maybe it was a vast cosmic explosion caused by a star in a near-collision with Earth, or the impact of a big meteor, or even the huge eruption of a volcano. Whatever it was produced a thick canopy of smoke and dust around the world which cut the power of the sun and drastically lowered the temperature, so that a climate that had been warm and wet became dry and cold. Vast inland formations of glacier ice began to cover huge portions of the northern hemisphere, and as the sea water froze into glaciers, the very oceans began to dry up, exposing wide new beaches. When the level of the Bering Sea went down, a land-bridge joining Siberia with Alaska was left high and dry, growing shrubs and grass with vast expanses of sedge meadows in the low places. Thus it became a natural crossing between the two continents for a flow of grazing animals: hairy mammoths, woolly rhinoceroses, giant bison, antelopes, horses, camels, several kinds of deer, bears, wolves, and several giant cats, including the sabre-toothed tiger and the great cave lion. Following these animals on their trek from Asia into North America – an empty land – came man.

What is scientifically known as Beringia reached from northern-central Europe across Asia into North America in a linked series of great open refugiums, where the ice did not come except in advancing and receding thrusts of intrusions. The land where the Oldman now runs was especially important in those days, since it was relatively dry all year round, and rimmed to the east and west by mile-deep glacier ice. The climate was dry, varying between cold, fierce winters laced with blizzards and raging winds, and warm summers perhaps even warmer than today. This land was a kind of steppe covered with long grass for the most part, with low shrubbery of various kinds for grazing animals on which predators preyed.

The most powerful of these was man. Originally he had been naked in the southern country where he had evolved, but now he had learned to clothe himself in the skins of animals bearing fur and wool. He was a very efficient big-game hunter armed with a spear, which he threw from the hand, and very probably with the help of throwing-sticks known as atlatyls. Spear points were made from stone, ivory, and probably antlers, and so were knives, scrapers, awls, and sewing needles. The beautifully worked stone points, totally indestructible by weather and passing time, have left an indelible record of man's presence and marked his trails like ageless blazes.

Today's investigating scientists, searching for those trails, occasionally find the old campsites, though a vast majority of them are deep under an overburden of earth, where discovery so far is largely accident. When they do come across one of these old hunting camps, the evidence is rich and unmistakably written in ashes, charcoal, and bone and ivory fragments, and tells a story of what was hunted and how long ago. For by the carbon crystal process and other even more sophisticated means, the age of these artifacts can be estimated accurately, give or take a few hundred years. Animal blood and tissue on spear points, incorporated by natural chemicals into the stone, can also be read, so that even the species killed can be identified. We know that the earliest North Americans lived in lodges constructed of hides laid over poles or mammoth ribs. Sometimes they utilized caves, and their favourite prey was the mammoths.

These huge animals were a part of the elephant species. As we have seen, the bulls grew enormous curving ivory tusks that could reach a length of sixteen feet, while the females had shorter and straighter tusks. They were all fully covered with brown hair, mainly three feet long but much shorter on legs and feet, which overlaid thick wool, heavy hide, and several inches of subcutaneous fat. Highly specialized animals, they had smaller ears but thicker and shorter trunks than those of today's elephants. The bulls were about twelve feet high at the shoulders, with backs sloping to the hindquarters, while the cows were somewhat smaller. They all ate enormously of grass and shrubbery. Slow breeders, they were also very selective feeders and thus were vulnerable to heavy hunting pressure and changing times, which ultimately caused them to vanish from North America, along with many other animals too specialized to survive. But they deeply marked an epoch of importance in our history, for the men who hunted them were the forebears of our present-day native people.

It was one thing for these spear-throwing hunters to go out after bison, or the original type of horses, deer, and other desirable animals. But unless they were taken in numbers, such animals could not long satisfy a camp full of hungry people. It was quite another thing to bag a big mammoth weighing about five or six live tons. Being so big and heavy, these animals were vulnerable to natural traps such as bogs or cliff-walled passages leading over passes from one feeding-ground to another. When conditions were favourable, the hunters no doubt herded them, using fire or other means, into such places, where they could be killed with greater safety. But where such traps were not available, they had to be taken by stalking until they were within range of the deadly throwing-spears.

If a thrown spear struck a rib squarely, it would just bounce back, doing little damage, but if it went between the ribs, it would penetrate deep enough to reach the lungs or the heart. No doubt these men knew anatomy well, and also aimed high on the flank to reach the kidneys or forward from behind the rib-cage to the liver, where heavy hemorrhaging soon brought the animal down. Then, the excitement and danger over, it was a matter of hard work.

Picture, if you can, a group of hunters standing, leaning on their spears, looking at the dead carcass of a recently killed bull. They have been through a hard fight, the effects of adrenalin in their blood are sloping off, and they are catching their breath as they soberly contemplate the task of butchering thousands of pounds of tissue, hide, and bone. Even with extra help from camp, it is a monumental task. To an average modern-day hunter equipped with the best steel knives, a saw, and an axe, it would appear, if not impossible, at least very daunting.

But these people know the quickest way to cut and loosen the hide. They are aware of how every muscle lies and how every joint is fastened. They are equipped with the keenest blades ever devised in the world and they know how to use them. They also have heavy stone axes for cutting heavy tendons and bones. When they swarm over that carcass, it begins to come apart like magic, till in a relatively short time it is reduced to piles of meat, fat, discarded bones, tusks, hide, and guts. Though certainly no stopwatch ever timed such an operation, a subsequent experiment using the same tools on the carcass of an African elephant was astonishingly successful.

These mammoth-hunters are now known among anthropologists as the Clovis Culture. They are so named for their distinctive and highly effective spear points made of flint knapped into very sharp points and edges, with shallow longitudinal grooves to couch the split end of the spear shaft on either side. Bound to the shaft with strips of wet rawhide, the points were held as in the jaws of a vice when the rawhide dried and shrank.

Those flint-knappers of ten to thirty thousand years ago were not just satisfied to make practical, usable tools, they embellished them with refinements that displayed the pride of the individual craftsman. Suitable stone was not common, and when a flint deposit was discovered, they no doubt stocked up with rough flakes stored in bags for their own use as well as trade. Probably one of the most desirable materials sought by the flint-knappers was the jet-black volcanic glass known as obsidian, which not only made superb points but also made knives with edges keener than the sharpest of modern steel scalpels. Generally these were triangular in shape, sometimes with two edges. Some were bound to handles of wood, ivory, or bone, but some were held in the fingers for more dextrous use. They were of such incredible keenness that modern manufacturers of surgical tools are duplicating them, using obsidian for specialized use.

Deposits of obsidian are rare, but there is a huge one in Yellowstone Park. Proof that it was mined and widely used in trade is verified by the finding of points made of this distinctive material all over western North America.

Beringia was a huge reservoir supporting great numbers of animals all directly or indirectly nurtured by the rich herbage: grass, lichen, moss, shrubs, and scrub trees. The earliest people, being omnivorous, not only ate the meat of the herbivores, but also fed on fresh fruit, roots, and green stuff in season. From the very beginning, they picked, dried, and stored seeds, nuts, berries, herbs, and roots for use outside the growing season. Though they no doubt used nature's deep-freeze in the permafrost, as well as caves cut into the ever-present ice, to preserve their meat, they also no doubt knew how to dry and smoke it. A hunter can easily carry enough of this jerky to keep him well supplied with protein for a considerable journey.

The two major ice sheets that periodically ebbed and flowed in North America during the Ice Age were the Laurentian to the east and the Cordilleran to the west. The former was perhaps the biggest, covering a vast area that stretched to the east coast and south to the general region and latitude of Kansas. The Cordilleran mountain glacier straddled the Continental Divide from Alaska to

Colorado, great jagged peaks like fangs of rock protruding from it here and there.

For a long period during the time of the great ice, these two continental glaciers never really met, but left an open refugium reaching from eastern Beringia down through Alberta south to the open ground. Thus, the area I plan to talk about was the continent's main highway, a beckoning trail leading animals and men toward the sun.

There was never a real exodus; probably small groups of people just took off from their northern camps and never showed up again. Or maybe some of them did. We can imagine young hunters, perhaps sixteen- and seventeen-year-olds, salty and feeling their oats under a warm spring sun, banding together in a small group to set out on a great journey. They could have easily made it through to the southern rim of the ice-fields in two seasons, hunting as they went and perhaps camping with others of their kind. Then, after a period of hunting and living in a warmer clime, they would get restless to see the folks back north – perhaps they even remembered a girl – and set out to retrace their steps. Arriving back as fully developed hunters, they could enthrall their audiences with tales of their adventures in a far-off land beyond the ice, thus sparking the imaginations of other youngsters to do the same.

As primitive hunters throughout the world have always been, the Beringians of that early culture were no doubt highly spiritualistic. They could not help relating to the great animals that they hunted, and in the course of their lives must have experienced many highly dramatic occurrences for which they had no explanation. Earthquakes doubtless shook the ground under their feet at times, for there is always movement and tension in the continental plate, which would be accelerated by the enormous burden of ice.

These masses of ice would be continuously in motion, and this movement is always accompanied by periodic booming, creaking, groaning, and cracking. Anyone who has watched the calving front of a great glacier in surge, tall towers of blue ice falling thunderous-

ly into a river or over a cliff, will never forget the awesome sight.
And there was always the aurora borealis, the northern lights shimmering and dancing at night across the sky to the accompaniment of
hissing and swishing noises that made the watcher's skin prickle.
No man of that time, when nature was flexing its muscles, could
live without becoming influenced by spiritual beliefs.

These people were hunters and questers whose trails took them
far south through North America and then on down the length of
South America to its farthest tip. But not all at once, or in a short
period of time like the sudden intrusion of Europeans into North
America, where they first encountered the descendants of these
people and called them savages. We have just barely, within the last
century, found enough evidence to confirm that this gradual spread
of hunters from the north happened at all.

At one dig near where Taber, Alberta, now stands in the region
described by this book, part of the skeleton of a girl has been found
dating from 40,000 years ago. Other sites of great antiquity show
the pattern of inhabited locations in North America scattered over
such a wide area that the discoveries amount only to picking up
little straws of significant evidence from what is a continental hay-
stack. They can be recorded as follows in brief: Shequiandah,
Ontario, 30,000 years; American Falls, Idaho, 40,000 years; Los
Angeles, California, 23,600 years; Santa Rosa Island, California,
30,000 years; Tlapacoya, Mexico, 22,000 years; and Valseqillo,
Mexico, 22,000 years. All of them are based on data concerned with
locations where skeletal remains of man have been found, in addition to the northernmost site, at Old Crow Flats in the Yukon
Territory, which has been dated at 25,000 years ago.

But in the meantime, down south of the ice, these people of the
old Clovis Culture had wandered far and wide from the heavily
forested Atlantic shore to the Pacific coast. They had moved on
south as well through Central America into South America, which
had its own Ice Age of a lesser degree, where the distinctive Clovis

spear points have marked their path clear into Patagonia, at the tip of South America.

We also know for certain that they crossed and camped and hunted and lived on the ground that is now the location of the valley of the Oldman River here in southern Alberta, at a time when its waters had not yet started to run.

2 The Early Americans

Having been a hunter who has known what it means to support my family with wild meat and the money from furs taken along rough mountain trails, there is no doubt in my mind why man moved eastward from Asia across the land-bridge into North America. He was a hunter and gatherer, too, and he trailed with his prey. Being a "yondering" type, with an abiding curiosity that led him up the creek and over the hill to see what might be hidden on the other side, he was of a mind to follow his nose into the wind, cutting the sign of the animals he liked to eat and on occasion moving his family to newly discovered hunting-grounds. When they moved, these people did not go very quickly, for they carried everything on their backs, so their drifting was not very dramatic; it just happened. Because of the close proximity of millions upon millions of cubic miles of ice flanking the open regions of Beringia, they were cold a good part of the time, and understandably restless, for such a climate does not breed laziness.

After crossing Alaska and the Yukon through miles and miles of rich savannah dotted with clumps of brush and trees, upon which their favourite prey, the mammoths, fed, they inevitably came to the open refugium flanked by the two major ice masses of the continent. When they followed this southward through what is now Alberta into what we know as the United States, they came out into the great parklands and forests covering the country south of the ice sheets. On this journey through the refugium, they were rarely out of sight of the ice to the east and the west, which was almost two miles deep in places. This was savannah country, too, with swamps and lakes. Because it was confined, it made for good hunting, for their prey animals could go only two ways; no animals ventured up onto the ice, except to cross spurs that projected here and there into the corridor.

It must have been an almost overwhelming experience to reach the limitless reaches of parkland and forest, where cold, milky rivers flowed and the climate was much more salubrious. Here the animals spread out ahead of them, and the various small parties of people lost themselves. Their trails fanned out across the land, while they learned new techniques and doubtless enjoyed an easier way of life.

Over the thousands of years of the Ice Age the great masses of the Appalachian and Cordilleran ice ebbed and flowed, the last great surge of the ice coming about 12,000 years ago. It closed the refugium and cut off any movement of life southward from Beringia.

As the climate began to moderate, warm winds began to carve away at the masses of ice to the north. Great lakes began filling the basins between stranded moraines of rock and silt, and the hollows gouged out in the solid bedrock of the land soon brimmed with water. These lakes ultimately spilled over, and streams of water rushed away seeking lower ground. Thus, over time, huge rivers came to cut out their valleys, the Mississippi, the Hudson, and the St. Lawrence among them, all fed by the tremendous volumes of meltwater unlocked from the ice and now finding its way back to the oceans. The Salmon and the Snake, the Columbia and the Fraser, along with their many tributaries, spilled west off the slopes of the Continental Divide as the land was uncovered to the north.

The summers were hot, accompanied day and night by the mighty roar of water. No doubt the floods claimed many lives as animals and men were caught in horrendous spills as natural dikes gave way. But the winters were cold; a time when the retreating ice came to a stand. It took a long time, but each succeeding summer the sun renewed its battle with the ice, laying bare more land to the accompaniment of roaring floods. Generations of men watched, while this great fight between the sun and the ice went on. Meanwhile, they hunted and gathered as always, although their prey changed.

It has always been an inexorable rule that suitable habitat is the key to survival of all animals, including man. If destructive changes proceed beyond a certain time limit, the end result is the same – an inevitable wipe-out. The climatic alterations occurring in a relatively short time transformed the habitat of the mammoths. These big animals, along with others like the mastodons, woolly rhinoceroses, long-horned bison, ground sloths, camels, and horses, to name a few, found themselves unable to adjust and consequently disappeared in North America.

It is not known when man first began organizing the mass slaughter of bison and other animals in natural traps such as box canyons, by driving them into corrals made of logs or stone, or by stampeding them over the edge of a steep bluff. At the Olsen Chubhuck site in Colorado, some two hundred long-horned bison skeletons have been found on the stone floor of a steep-sided draw. They had all been systematically butchered, except for thirteen skeletons found whole on the bottom of the pile, which the hunters obviously couldn't reach in time to make food of the carcasses. The last of these long-horned bison died out about 9,000 years ago and were much larger than those we know today. I was once given a long-horned buffalo skull dug out of the blue silt of the Milk River not very far from where it crosses out of Montana into Alberta. Except for the missing lower jaw and horn shells, it was intact. It measured thirty-six inches across the bone cores supporting the horns – not the horns, the supporting bone cores! They were obviously big animals, probably weighing at least twice as much as their successors.

These prehistory people were by no means totally dependent on meat for their food. Scientists have found indisputable evidence of the use of fruit and seed supplements to their diet, along with fragments of hair and insects. They have made these discoveries by microscopic examination of their fossil excrement; this is the study of what are known as coprolites, a very positive way of identifying what passed through the digestive systems of people ages ago.

Of course, nothing is known of their language; what they talked about, or the stories they told around their campfires will forever be a mystery. Nor do we know anything of the depth of their spiritualism, but because they lived among dramatic surroundings exposed to natural phenomena very difficult for them to understand, it is reasonable to believe that they would relate them to the spirit world. And we do know, from their descendants' beliefs, that the power of the sun was of great spiritual importance to their lives.

So far very little of their art has been found except the distinctive stonework involved with the weapons and tools of the Clovis Culture people, and the Fulsom Culture people who succeeded them, and who made scrapers, awls, spokeshaves, drills, knives, and projectile points as lovely as jewellery. There is one sample of a bit of charred weaving that may be a part of a basket found in Meadowcraft, a rock shelter on a small tributary of the Ohio River not far from Pittsburgh, that dates from more than 19,000 years ago. This makes it second in age to a hide scraper, made from the leg bone of a caribou down the Porcupine River north of Old Crow in the Yukon, which is approximately 27,000 years old. Because these prehistory hunters were nomadic survivors rather than builders, there have been no temples unearthed with paintings on their walls like those in France's Caves at Lascaux, 20,000 years old, or equally illustrative ones found in Brazil. The Bluefish Springs Caves dig in the Yukon is barren of such records. Maybe these hunters – like their prairie descendants – practised their art on hides, and, sadly, leather is fragile stuff.

At some point during the dramatic thousand-year retreat of the ice, or shortly after, when the climate was warming up fast, the bow and arrow appeared in North America as a major weapon. Before then, Clovis man's chief technical innovation had been the spear-thrower, a stick about the length of a forearm with a socketed hook at one end to hold the butt of the spear shaft. Steadying and point-ing the spear with the other hand, the hunter could rear back and, extending the leverage of his throwing arm, put his whole body into the throw. When tangling with an enraged mammoth, this was a decided advantage.

The bow was an even greater advantage. Originally invented in the Near East – and Harold Horwood in his book *Dancing On The Shore* has speculated whether even a genius like Einstein could have invented the bow and arrow – it was then widely adopted in the Orient and in Europe. It is uncertain whether the bow was re-invented in North America or introduced by Orientals who drifted across to the western shore of this continent on boats or rafts, but it became a very effective hunting and fighting weapon that changed the lives of the native people who mastered this new technology.

At around the same time as the arrival of the bow and arrow dur-ing the Big Melt, a river was born. This river was to become a focal point of not only the geography but also the history of what is now southern Alberta, as well as being destined to become of great spir-itual significance to the native people in the region as their holy river.

Just east of the Rockies in the region of the Porcupine Hills, the two great glacial ice sheets had met in collision. At one place the glacier from the west had ripped through the ridge of the Living-stone Range, swinging in a sharp curve around the north side of Thunder Mountain. Now the hills were bare, softly curving in their contours, and within the mountains the valleys were U-shaped from the ploughing of the ice. Above the valleys, high in the mountains, the meltwater hung up in a great lake trapped by stranded moraines. Finally it broke through on the eastern side, and through the glacier-created gap at the foot of Thunder Mountain came a river busily carving a channel down across the rocky plain, curving southward around the end of the Porcupine Hills. It was to be called the Oldman River by the tribesmen who came to occupy this uncovered new land.

A few miles down it was joined by two more rivers boisterously making their way eastward from the mountains, the Crowsnest and the Castle. Farther east, the Belly, the St. Mary's, and the Waterton came in from the south, and the icy Bow from the northwest to form the South Saskatchewan, soon joined by the Red Deer from the north. In turn, at the Forks just east of today's Prince Albert, the combined rivers join with the North Saskatchewan to form the Saskatchewan running into Lake Winnipeg and from there northeast to Hudson Bay, and eventually into the Atlantic.

It is interesting to note that the rain that falls in the Oldman watershed ends up in the Atlantic. Raindrops from the same storm that fall a mile to the west will flow down the western slopes to the Pacific, while those that fall a mile to the south, draining into the Milk River in southern Alberta, will reach the Mississippi, and eventually the Gulf of Mexico. It is a land of ambitious rivers, none more historic or beautiful than the Oldman, with its tributaries coming into it like small vessels feeding an artery that carries the lifeblood of the land. Down the east slope of the Divide from the bases of great mountains – Tornado, Gould's Dome, Beehive, and Gass Peak – it winds its way from the timberline bighorn-sheep pastures across lovely flower-strewn flats where elk, deer, buffalo, and moose feed. Grizzlies and black bears graze on the lush growth, eat berries, and dig ground squirrels.

Over the years, fish came up from Hudson Bay, populating these rivers with teeming millions of cut-throat trout, Dolly Varden char, Rocky Mountain whitefish, redfin suckers, and others. The Oldman, being less precipitous than other mountain rivers, with pools and runs in abundance, was a piscatorial heaven from end to end. Beavers dammed the smaller side-streams, and as they cut down the trees, other generations of growth replaced the groves. So the valley of the Oldman was one long, self-renewing ecological garden overflowing with life, set among mountains and hills of unsurpassed beauty.

So it was when the descendants of the Clovis and Fulsom people found it. The first ones were pit-dwellers fashioning their shelters by digging holes in the ground and roofing them with poles and earth. Not very much is known about these tribesmen, for very few of their camps have been found, although I know one – tragically destroyed – close beside the Oldman only a few miles from its source. We know much more about the people who followed, who lived in skin tipis made of bison hides pitched over a cone of poles. These were the Shoshoni or Snake, the Kutenai, the Gros Ventre, the Sarcee, the Stoney, and the Blackfoot tribes that we know today.

3 *Where the Wind Blows Free*

While we depend to some extent on old legends passed down through generations of our native peoples, we have ample proof of their presence on the plains and mountain country of western Canada. We also know that they were on foot when they moved and that somewhere along the back trails of their history they had acquired dogs for packing and dragging loads. They were nomadic, and while they lived in certain geographic locations there were no boundaries to their territories, for they followed the buffalo, the major source of their food. When they strayed into territories claimed by other tribes there could be conflict, depending on the circumstances: their reactions in any given situation were largely governed by the phase of the moon, dreams, and many other subtle yet very real signs and signals. Consequently, if two strong parties from enemy tribes met, there could be a temporary amnesty.

In these very early times, the Shoshoni pitched their tipis in the valley of the Oldman River. They were a powerful tribe, buffalo Indians accustomed to living and hunting on the arid plains. At the same time, the Kutenai tribe occupied a territory that reached right across the Rocky Mountains from the valley of the river that still bears their name all the way to the edge of the plains country at the foot of their eastern slope, sometimes overlapping Shoshoni territory in the Oldman country. To the north, around the North Saskatchewan, the Blackfoot Indians occupied a region in the parkland country, and to the northeast, where the trees and prairies met, were the Gros Ventre.

These tribes were different in their physical features and their dress, and also spoke different languages. But basically they were the same, children of the wilderness following the rules of their spiritual beliefs, living under the all-powerful sun. The Kutenais and the Shoshonis on occasion camped east of the hills on the Oldman River. When they found the need to go upstream through the gap cut by the glacier around Thunder Mountain, where the river's clear waters foamed around big boulders and showed deep blue in the pools, they paid homage to the Great Spirit – the Old Man – by ceremoniously placing a rock on a pile located on a point overlooking the sweep of the valley. It was a sort of token paid for entering the Old Man's country, for they believed that the great spirit lived here among the peaks where the river began. It was a ritual carried out by the first people who saw this place and was religiously followed by all who came after, until the pile of rocks grew to be enormous.

Whether by sickness or through war, the Shoshonis were weakened and retreated southward from this portion of the western plains, leaving it to the Blackfoot tribe, who were also enemies of the Kutenais and began to put pressure on them. Not as numerous as the Blackfoot Nation, which was made up of Southern Blackfoot, Northern Blackfoot, Blood, Peigan, and Sarcee, the Kutenais were finally defeated in a great battle and retreated through the passes leading over the Continental Divide and down to the Tobacco Plains along the Kootenay River that we know today.

Thus the Blackfoot tribe, which originally came from the plains and bush country to the northeast, became a real power on the plains, and the main power around the Oldman. Like all the tribes, they did not claim to own land, but they did lay claim to the right to use it. Legend has it that the Old Man gave the Blackfoot people a great hunting-ground that reached from the North Saskatchewan River south to the Musselshell, all along the hill and plains country east of the Rocky Mountains. They were instructed to guard it well, and this they did. Included in this vast stretch of country was the sacred Oldman River. When they had occasion to go through the Gap into the mountains that they feared, to camp, hunt, and, above all, cut new tipi poles, they also left their token stones on the pile.

For protection and success in the style of hunting they practised, they generally travelled in bands. In winter they established camps in sheltered valleys and generally remained there, depending on the availability of buffalo. In summer the bands moved from one place to another following the buffalo and also coming together for big celebrations, sun dances, games, and general pow-wows involved with war and hunting. Moving camp was a laborious undertaking for the women and the dogs, since everything the band owned had to be carried or dragged. Women carried loads almost as big as themselves. The dogs either carried packs or dragged small travois behind them, the butts of the poles trailing on the ground. When a big camp moved, hundreds of dogs were thus employed.

On the trail, these moves were well organized, with women, children, and old people in the centre and the warriors deployed ahead, on both flanks and to the rear, armed and ready for any trouble they might encounter. Scouts roamed all around. When a selected campground was reached, tipis were pitched and fires made with buffalo chips (dried dung) or wood; the all-important fire itself was carefully carried from camp to camp in a hollow horn lined with a slow-burning paste of the dampened powder of rotten wood. As the columns of smoke rose from the fires, such a camp, made up of a dozen – or two or three hundred – tipis, was an impressive sight in its wilderness setting.

The smallest political unit of the Blackfoot hierarchy was the band, which was an extended family. Each band was a self-sufficient group under a political chief who was commander of all movements in normal times; when war threatened, however, the war chief took control. The political chief took the role of chief magistrate, presiding as "chairman" of council meetings, settling disputes among members of the band, and instructing camp police. These police were selected from the warrior society, and were generally noted for their prowess with weapons, their physical stamina, and their skill as trackers. They acted as guardians during a buffalo hunt and protected the band on the trail, patrolling at night as well as during the day and scouting far and wide. When the chief passed sentence on an erring individual, they saw that it was carried out. A thief might be banished from camp, or a man who hunted alone and frightened the buffalo herds away might have all of his most valuable possessions confiscated.

On occasions when several bands joined in one camp, no one was the automatic head chief; instead, someone would be chosen to act while the bands stayed together. Council meetings were generally made up of the head chief, the war chief, and the heads of various families. The head chief practised great diplomacy, for he was dealing with individuals much too proud to be intimidated, who could walk out any time and separate their camps from the gathering. He relied on oratory to make known his feelings about an issue or a decision; then each councilman had his turn, and when at last the play of words ended, he knew where consensus lay and announced where he was going and what he was going to do; he gave no orders, but knew he would be followed.

The religion of the Blackfoot people was complicated, highly ritualistic, and full of much spiritual significance. Hugh A. Dempsey has written: "Religion pervaded every aspect of daily life. A woman beginning her quill working would say a prayer; an old man awaking in the morning would sing a prayer of thanks; a person before eating placed a small morsel of food on the ground for the spirits."

The Blackfoot believed that their entire universe was inhabited by spirits, some good (like most earth spirits) and some evil (like most water spirits). One of the greatest of these was the Sun, who was the head of a holy family consisting of his wife, the Moon, and their boy, the Morning Star. The thunder spirit was a powerful deity, while even a lowly mouse had its supernatural role. A strangely twisted tree or an unusual rock formation was considered to be the manifestation of spiritual power, and, as a result, passersby left offerings for good luck.

"Medicine bundles" consisted of sacred objects wrapped together and used for religious purposes. Some contained war shirts decorated with scalps or unusual skins; others had fossilized ammonites, known as buffalo stones, or other parts of costume. But most common of all was the medicine pipe, which was a long pipe-stem without a bowl, decorated with eagle feathers, that was used in dances to bring good luck or good health. Medicine bundles were contained within a large rawhide case which hung on a tripod behind the owner's lodge in the day and was carried inside to hang above his sleeping-place at night.

Medicine bundles also were used by various secret societies of the Blackfoot. And it should be noted that, although women did not normally take an active role in most societies, the Blackfoot were unique in that they had one society, the Motoki, exclusively for women; its primary function was to remind the people of the importance of buffalo to their way of life.

Buffalo were the major source of food, clothing, and much else. For thousands of years the Blackfoot hunted them by driving them in herds over the cliffs of the steep bluffs along the rivers in the foothills. Perhaps the most famous of these sites is Head-Smashed-In buffalo jump, which is now a provincial park in Alberta and is located on the north side of the Oldman River close by the Porcupine Hills. It was used by the Indians for thousands of years; indeed, it was used for so long that the old marks of the drives behind the jump are still visible from the air, even though the ground has been farmed now for many years.

These mass kills were very carefully planned, with rules that no hunter dared overlook. Long lines of blinds were built in a converg-

ing V leading to the top of the jump. These blinds were mounds of
rocks, buffalo chips, or brush – whatever material was handy – and
were just big enough to hide a man. When a buffalo herd grazed
into position beyond the open mouth of the V, the hunters took up
positions behind the blinds, while others circled around the herd,
showing themselves here and there to move them in the right direction. In the meantime, two or three fleet-footed young men dressed
in wolf skins crept out into the middle of the open wings of the V,
where they cavorted and danced around on hands and knees to at-
tract the curiosity of the nearest buffalo, drawing them into coming
for a closer look. If all went well, and the herd began moving into
the run, the hunters behind it came in closer, easing the stragglers
in the right direction until they were all moving steadily between
the wings of the blinds.

If the buffalo started to veer off to the side, the hunters behind
the blinds showed themselves to turn them back. As they passed the
blinds, the hunters stood up, waving robes and yelling and whooping to spook them, until finally the herd was running in full stampede, with the decoy wolves out in front bounding fast toward the
hidden edge of the jump-off. As the lines of the blinds converged,
the herd was compacted, with those in front pressed by those
behind, so that when they came to the edge of the cliff, the thundering mass of animals had no choice but to leap off into space, rolling and tumbling down in a great heaving heap. There the hunters
made short work of killing any that were still alive. It was a bloody,
wild, and totally successful method of slaughter, sometimes so
successful that it was wasteful, but it provided meat for a big camp
in a relatively easy fashion. With millions of buffalo roaming the
plains, such a kill had no more effect than a speck of dust on a dry
hillside.

Most of the time food was fairly easy to obtain. But sometimes,
when the winter camps were made up, as usual, along the sheltered
valleys in the hills, where the people could easily draw water from
the rivers like the Oldman, the buffalo remained far out on the open

plains. Then the Blackfoot knew starving conditions. In a nomadic culture, people on foot have no easy means of transporting or keeping meat, but depend on the animals coming to them. They did smoke and dry jerky, but this did not last very long. And only in times of the greatest starvation would they stoop to fishing in rivers like the Oldman. The Blackfoot were never fish-eaters.

Girls were instructed by their mothers to do simple chores, helping to gather firewood and carry water. The boys were shown by an older brother, or an uncle, how to make and use bows and arrows and other weapons, and how to follow tracks and hunt. When a boy made his first kill of a grouse or a rabbit, his father announced this feat in a loud voice all through the camp. At twelve or thirteen years, boys were often given a name by older brothers that was so disparaging that it encouraged them to go to war to earn an adult name. On these first expeditions, they were servants, tending fires, cooking, repairing moccasins, and doing any other lesser jobs required of them. They usually did not fight, but if they did well, they could win their warrior's name.

When a young man reached a marriageable age, he would court a girl by being close to her path as she went to gather wood or get water, or near her tipi at night. The object, as in our society, was to be noticed at every opportunity. But clandestine contact was not encouraged by the girls' parents, for virginity was held in high esteem and had religious significance. In fact, the Blackfoot had a very rigid moral code and were highly modest. Even in the hottest summer weather, the men always wore a breech-clout and the women a dress, which they could untie on the sides from the waist down. Courting was carried out with considerable decorum.

Marriage arrangements depended a good deal on the wealth and social status of the families. A poor boy could indenture himself to his father-in-law by agreeing to work for him for a given length of time. In any event, the parents of the participants worked out the details. Usually, the bride moved to her husband's camp with a dowry of a new tipi and furnishings. These remained her belongings, and if for some reason there was a separation, she retained ownership. Polygamy was common, and the number of wives depended on a man's ability to support them. Sometimes a man married sisters. The first wife, however, was the one in charge of the female household, and she was known as the "sits beside him" woman, who attended feasts and ceremonies with the husband. Polyandry—a wife sharing several husbands—was not unknown, though death from war and hunting among the men made this uncommon.

If a woman was unfaithful, the husband generally took her back to her father and demanded the return of the gifts he had given for her. Similarly, if she found him to be cruel and a poor provider, she could leave him. If a bride got homesick and went back to her camp, she was promptly sent back by her parents, who had no desire to be made to look as though they had raised a frivolous daughter.

The wives had a hard life. In addition to carrying all the equipment on the trail, they were relegated to patching tents, butchering and curing meat, tanning hides, cooking, making and decorating clothing, as well as general maintenance of the tipi, and training the girls. The men were the hunters; they protected the camp, made weapons and their own clothing, and went on raids of enemy camps. The decoration of the outside of the lodge was done by the men, while the women painted the interior lining as well as the furnishings. When a man was dying, he was dressed in his best clothes, with all his personal gear placed around him. Upon his death, he was not buried but was placed on a platform in a tree or on posts set in the ground. Sometimes he was left in the tipi when he died. The camp was always abandoned, for the Blackfoot believed his spirit would haunt the area.

A woman mourned the death of a husband by cutting off her hair, slashing her legs, and sometimes even amputating a finger at the joint. She wailed in ritualistic chant, and such mourning went on periodically for about a year.

Tipis were generally made from the skins of two-year-old cow buffalo, as the hides of mature animals were very heavy. A well-made lodge, cone-shaped and fitting the poles smoothly without any wrinkling or sagging when properly pitched, not only resisted the wind but was also rainproof. A tipi is one of the simplest yet most efficient engineering designs ever invented by man. When laid out flat on the ground it formed a half-circle. Slung around the poles, it came together perfectly from the smoke-hole down to the top of the door, where it was buttoned by wooden fasteners. The outside edge was staked down with pins, sometimes made of the shin-bones of deer. Flaps of hide were fastened to the skirt to lay out on the ground, with rocks placed on them as insurance against the wind. The ears of the smoke flaps were hung on two extra poles so that they could be adjusted to the direction of the wind and opened or closed according to the weather. Perhaps the most amazing thing of all about the tipi was how the women cut the pattern from the skins and sewed them together so they could be pitched perfectly, regardless of size; a mind-boggling undertaking for anyone un-schooled in the artistry required.

There was a good deal of competition among the women and men in the colourful decoration of ceremonial clothing by the skilful sewing of dyed porcupine quills to the soft smoke-tanned skins from elk, moose, and deer. Such garments were also enhanced by fringes of various lengths. Some clothing for very special occasions was made from snow-white unsmoked hides, and these were guarded carefully from rain, as they would shrink from being wet.

The men's colourful and symbolic head-dresses, made of eagle feathers, were not made by the women, but were collected and manufactured by the men who wore them. The hunting of the great birds was very ingenious; the hunter would climb up to the top of a ridge, dig a pit big enough to hide in, and then cover himself with a fresh, bloody calf-buffalo skin, flesh side out. When a circling eagle spotted this decoy and swooped down to feed, the hidden brave would grab it by the legs and, evading the slashing beak, capture and kill it. One of the favourite places to hunt eagles was up on the headwaters of the Oldman River, where the big birds swung on the thermals over the craggy peaks and ridges.

There was scarcely a part of a deer, a wild sheep, or a buffalo that these people did not use for something. The thin strips of cartilege covering the loin muscles were dried and stripped into the sinew strands used for sewing. Horn, when softened by boiling, can be straightened and easily worked with scrapers and shavers. Buffalo horn came in for many uses. The horns of bighorn rams were used to make very efficient ladles and spoons. Buffalo leg skins with the dew claws attached were fashioned into rattles worn on the ankles of dancers to accompany their movements. Rawhide stretched over a hollowed-out section of a log was the drum most commonly used to accompany these dancers, with its compelling, mesmerizing sound.

Most dances were for men only and depicted hunting and war, and they were generally accompanied by singers lifting their voices in high cadence in rhythm with the drums. Some dances were copies of animal and bird behaviour, like the Prairie Chicken Dance, which was adapted from the mating dance of this grouse. Other dances were for women only, and some, like the Owl Dance, were for both sexes, when the women selected their partners. Bravery in battle, success in hunting, mourning, and just pure joy were all depicted by the many dances and songs, and few sights could be as impressive and of such dramatic impact as these people dressed in their colourful clothing moving in cadence under the warm sun or at night in the light of fires.

All this was seen by the Oldman in the summer and winter camps built along its banks, long before the coming of the first white men, and their assumptions that they were exploring a land without history.

4 *Horse and Buffalo*

What had been a way of life for thousands of years began feeling the first touch of the winds of change; for the horse had come back to North America in the ships of Spanish explorers, who were settling in Mexico. Where the Blackfoot first encountered the horse is something hidden by time, but it almost certainly occurred to the south. Legend has it that a party of Blackfoot warriors was attacked by a party of mounted Shoshonis, who suddenly swooped in on them firing their arrows from horseback, to the utter amazement and no doubt embarrassment of these fierce tribesmen. It is not difficult to imagine the excitement and dismay back in camp when the Blackfoot warriors returned with their stories of this big medicine of the Shoshonis. The news no doubt was carried fast to every camp in the Blackfoot hunting country by the moccasin telegraph. Since there was no word for horse in their language, they may have identified this amazing animal by calling them "medicine dogs", or something akin to the only domesticated animal they knew.

Some time between 1700 and 1725, however, the Blackfoot acquired horses. How they obtained them is not known, but it was likely by trade, perhaps with the Mandans to the southeast on the Missouri River, who knew about and traded with the Spanish. All it would take to give them a start in raising horses would be a stallion and a couple of mares, for they lived on the finest kind of horse range in the entire world. In a relatively short time the Blackfoot were mounted, and the cultural change in their lives was instant.

Now they found themselves incredibly mobile, able to move easily from place to place; journeys that once took weeks were now possible in a few days, and when they arrived, they were fresh and ready for anything. Always fierce and proud in their bearing, the men now had that certain arrogance that goes with sitting tall on the back of a horse. No longer did the women have to labour over the prairies on foot when they moved camp, carrying back-breaking loads. The tipi poles made fine travois, enabling her to ride the horse that pulled a much bigger load. Extra possessions were packed on the backs of other horses, for now they counted their wealth in horses.

Now tipis could be made bigger, requiring twelve to fourteen buffalo skins and as many as twenty-three lodge poles. Some wealthy men had lodges that were palatial, sewn from thirty skins, and with two doors and two fireplaces. They were constructed in two pieces, each forming a single travois load. To anyone who has had experience putting up a tipi, pitching such a lodge was an amazing feat of ingenuity, for they were about thirty feet high and required about thirty-two poles of sufficient length. It was here that the advantages of having at least four wives to do the necessary work became very evident! Such a lodge-owner's status in the hierarchy of the band as a hunter, leader, or warrior was assured, and marked him as having done something outstanding in war.

With a little imagination we can see this man at night, reclining against a willow back-rest, telling stories to visiting relatives and friends, eating and smoking with them while the flames from the fires lit up the towering cone of poles overhead in golden hues. The liner, tied on the inside of the poles to a head-high level, decorated with designs and figures painted by the women, made a colourful backdrop. Up through the smoke-hole a bright star looked down, while outside, a favourite horse or two, tied close by, occasionally stamped and whinnied gently. It was very pleasant, and even the dogs must have enjoyed the new life, for now only the poorest people still used them as beasts of burden.

But wealth generates envy, and now the Blackfoot warriors were at war much of the time. The Crees to the north were hungry to acquire horses and came to raid their herds, along with the Assiniboines, and both tribes wished to hunt on their buffalo-rich hunting-grounds. When the Blackfoot were not out driving away these intruders from the north, they were busy raiding the horse-rich Crows and Shoshonis to the south. Occasionally they tangled with the mighty Sioux to the southeast, whose descendants were to teach General Custer a terrible lesson.

The Blackfoot went to war either to capture enemy horses and other possible loot, or for revenge. A raiding party of young warriors would usually go on foot, sometimes for very long distances, to an enemy village, with considerable risk of discovery. Carefully they would prowl around the outskirts to discover where the horse herd grazed, and how many guards were in attendance, and to learn the details of the ground. Then, at the darkest point in the night, the warriors crept in close. It was no easy task to elude the guards, get in among the horses, and proceed to catch mounts, for horses are skittish and noisy in the darkness. But sometimes a daring and skilful young man would sneak up on a dozing guard, cut the lead rope of his horse, and lead it away without his being aware of it until too late. When everybody had a horse, they vaulted up onto their backs, and with fiendish yells shattered the stillness of the night to stampede the whole herd into a wild run.

They almost never got them all, so it wasn't long before pursuing enemy riders were hot on their trail. Then it was a race through the night, and the dawn, and on through the daylight hours, the pursued trying to keep the herd together and the pursuers doing their best to catch up. The Blackfoot were noted for their ability to keep stolen horses from scattering, thus depriving their enemies of rela-

tively fresh mounts. If they contrived to hold their horses together
for the first day, they had a distinct advantage, for by that time they
knew which horses were the leaders and which ones were the most
likely to break back. When darkness fell, they could change direction, thus slowing up pursuit, for it is almost impossible to trail
even a large number of horses at night. After a long run, a loose
bunch of driven horses is easier to manage, and with luck even half a
dozen well-mounted riders can put them anywhere they wish them
to go. With some luck in the general geography of the country and
perhaps a downpour of rain to erase the tracks, they could get away
from their pursuers. When they finally arrived back at their home
camp, it was time to celebrate. Young men who had left more or
less in poverty could come back rich, with the means of making
gifts for the hand of the girl of their dreams.

Much honour could be gained at home by a young raider who
could sneak in alone among enemy tipis at night and get away with
two or three choice mounts tied near their owner's lodge without
having to kill anyone. It was not considered necessary to kill an
enemy; to touch him with a pipe or a coup stick and get away with
his horses was far more daring. To collect a scalp for a trophy was a
secondary thing. It was a game for the youngsters eager to make a
name for themselves and to acquire some horses. Most warriors retired from it before reaching middle age to raise papooses and to
look after their horses.

When, for reasons of revenge, it was decided to mount a big
attack on an enemy tribe, the campaign was very carefully planned
by the war chief and his councillors. He could call on any camp for
men, and when he took the lead on his favourite war horse, he
might have two or three hundred superbly mounted men with him,
all rigged with their best weapons. Surprise was always something
they strove to have in their favour as they swooped in to attack. But
that was not always possible, for a large party of warriors was hard to
conceal. Quite often they found themselves facing an equally strong
war party, and it was then that great feats of daring sometimes un-

folded in the clouds of dust stirred up by whirling, plunging horse-men bent on killing adversaries. To show their bravery, some warriors would sometimes ride out between the opposing lines, dis-mount, and tie themselves with a short piece of rope to a stake driven in the ground. There they would stay until killed or until the enemy was defeated, defiantly staging their fight on foot within the confines of the tether.

Such set-piece battles were always wild and often bloody, often with heavy casualties. When the Blackfoot warriors returned to their camps, there was generally wailing of wives mourning husbands and relatives lost in such battles. All bodies of dead warriors were brought back if possible, and, following the funeral ceremonies, the camp was abandoned. It must have been a melancholy moment for the surviv-ing warriors to look back and see the burial platforms, or perhaps the lodges containing the bodies of their friends, with dead horses, their favourite mounts, stretched out alongside, and to hear the wailing of their women, sad under the prairie sun.

The wounded from such a battle were cared for with skill, for these people knew how to treat wounds and set broken bones and splint them with rawhide to hold them until they healed. Their knowledge of medicinal herbs and the roots of certain plants, picked from the foothill slopes and prairies or the banks of the Oldman, was extensive. They had medicine for just about every ailment they knew. The women had potions for birth control and abortions, and skilled individuals among them acted as midwives administering to difficult births. For the most part, the women had little trouble having babies and generally were up and going about their duties the very same day.

They were children of the earth. This was the golden era of the Blackfoot people, rich with horses and endowed with hordes of buf-falo in a hunting country so big that to climb a hill and look was to see forever. Vengeful and fierce as they could be, they were also sen-sitive to the world of the spirits and had a full understanding of the world in which they lived. They were the product of a dramatic prehistoric time covering eons of uncounted winters; their time of destiny was now, their position unchallenged as among the most attractive and free of all Stone Age cultures.

It was during this time of horse-raiding and hard riding that a daring raiding-party of young Crows set out from a camp far to the south heading north. Nobody knows who their leader was, but he must have been something of an explorer as well as a man with a powerful urge to acquire Blackfoot horses. Probably travelling at night and sleeping by day in some well-hidden spot, he led them on foot close to five hundred miles. In the valley of the Oldman River not far from the slopes of the Porcupine Hills, they crept into a large camp of Peigans and proceeded to abscond with a bunch of their horses. But the Peigans discovered them in time to pursue them closely and cut off their escape route south, whereupon the Crows changed direction and headed west up the Middle Fork, probably hoping to get over the mountains into friendly Kutenai country. The pursuing Peigans caught up to them, however, near the foot of a precipitous cone-shaped mountain that jutted out on the edge of the valley.

There the Crows abandoned their horses, took to the cover of the boulder-strewn lower slopes of the peak, and fought the Peigans fiercely. Reinforced with more warriors, the Peigans threw a ring around the entire mountain, determined to wipe out these cheeky horse-thieves from the south. Unable to get out, the Crows climbed the mountain under a cover of mist that blew in on a north wind. The following morning was clear and the Peigans could see them moving around against the sky. After a short period of siege, some of the young Peigan warriors climbed the peak – only to find the enemy gone. The astonished Peigans believed that their enemies had changed themselves into crows to fly away. They called the mountain Crow's Nest, and so a Rocky Mountain pass, a lake, and a river running out of it acquired a name.

No longer was the famous Head-Smashed-In buffalo jump in regular use, for, with horses, the Blackfoot found that they could ride up close beside the big animals and bury their deadly arrows clear to the feathers. At first the buffalo must have been confused by contact with horses, but they rapidly came to fear and hate them. Hunting buffalo on horseback was exciting and often dangerous, for, as many braves and their horses discovered, buffalo were incredibly quick on their feet, and could whirl in the wink of an eye to catch a horse on their horns and toss it high over their backs. A good hunting horse had not only to keep its feet out of badger and gopher holes, when a stumble could mean death, but also to know when to dodge an angry charge.

Generally a group of hunters rode as close as possible to a grazing herd and then coursed them at a high gallop, and when it was over, dead buffalo were sometimes strung out for miles. When conditions were right and the size of the herd was manageable, mounted Indians could make a ring forcing the buffalo into a milling mass in the centre. Then they pressed in close, running the outside rim of the circle, firing their arrows into the panicked animals until there were no more to fire. Every man's arrows carried his personal mark, so when the hunt was over, the women, who always did the skinning and butchering, knew which dead animals were killed by their husbands. Yet this information was for reasons of claiming and bragging only; the meat itself was fairly distributed among the members of the whole camp. The hunters could claim the robes, but a good hunter often gave most of them away. The Blackfoot were a truly communal society.

When they came to the Oldman River valley in summer, it could be to afford the women the chance to pick berries, or it might be to meet with people of another band for a visit. Whatever the reason, it was always an opportunity for the braves to join in competitions of various kinds, like the wheel-and-arrow game. This was a simple game involving a little wheel made of willow, which was rolled past the contestant, who attempted to throw or shoot an arrow through it as it passed.

Since the Blackfoot were a very physical people proud of their strength, the youngsters as well as the mature warriors competed in all sorts of games, including foot-races and wrestling-matches.

There were two kinds of wrestling, one conducted between two contestants on the ground and the other from horseback. The latter was
the most spectacular, for in this kind of match the contestants rode
up to each other mounted bareback, grabbed hold and wrestled, and
the man who first touched the ground was the loser. The skill was
not all with the riders, but involved their horses as well, for the
wrestler mounted on a well-trained horse that moved one way or
another following the leg-pressure signals of the rider had a distinct
advantage. A tall, strong man who locked his toes inside the front
legs of his mount, with his legs gripping like a vice, was very difficult to dislodge.

But the sport that was most enjoyed by young and old alike was
horse-racing. The races were run on a straight-away course of about
a quarter-mile between the start and the finish line. The riders,
usually youths of light weight, wore only a breech-clout and carried
a quirt. Coming up to the start-line, they were off at a given signal,
whipping their mounts at every stride. Betting could be heavy between families or bands when two famous horses raced, and sometimes caused trouble, as in the famous race described in his book *My
Life as an Indian* by J. W. Schultz, when a disputed result between
Peigan and Kutenai champion horses almost resulted in a war.

Most peaceful were the dances. One of the most popular was one
called the Assiniboine dance, which involves only unmarried men
and women. The two separate groups sit and face each other, while
the parents play the drums and everyone sings the dancing song in
lively tempo. The dancers come to their feet, rising on tiptoe, then,
stepping in time to the drums, advance till they almost meet, then
retreat. Back and forth they go, gazing into each other's eyes flirta-
tiously. Like most Indian dances it is a long-winded affair, with
occasional breaks to eat and smoke. Finally there comes a climax,
when one or more of the girls flips her robe over her head and the
head of her partner, and thus shielded from view they kiss, to the
huge entertainment of the watchers, while the drums beat and the
singing grows louder.

The young man thus trapped was expected to give the girl a gift, sometimes as much as one or two horses, depending on how thrilled he was by her looks and the contact. Whatever the feeling, he was expected to give her something, even if it was only a plain bracelet or a cheap string of beads. The Peigans were always a romantic, fun-loving people among themselves, however fierce and unforgiving they and the other Blackfoot were in war.

Some time during the season of the golden leaves, winter camps were chosen. Their location was influenced by natural shelter from the winter winds for the tipis, the abundance of firewood, the condition of the grass for the horses, the number of buffalo in the area, and the easy availability of water. The river valleys offered these advantages, and while the long, twisting valley of the Oldman was a favourite place for the various bands of the Blackfoot, it was by no means exclusive. They rarely if ever chose the same place each winter, for that would kill out the grass and use up the dry firewood. A camp of a hundred tipis needed a lot of wood and buffalo chips for cooking and heating; while each spring's flood inevitably scattered driftwood along the length of the river, by itself this was not enough. Meanwhile the nearby grazing might have been destroyed by fire.

Prairie fires often burned off enormous stretches of country, leaving the hills and prairies blackened and abandoned by the buffalo until the new grass of spring attracted them back. While the Indians sometimes deliberately set fires to burn off old grass, usually the fires were ignited by lightning or by a spark from a campfire. A grass fire running before a hard wind is a fearsome thing, but the Blackfoot people had their own methods of escaping them, by running off to the side, crossing a river, or back-firing a wide enough strip of grass to protect their tents. Usually the smoke and glare of flames at night gave plenty of warning of an approaching fire and time for moving out from in front of it. A camp getting burned out was a rare occurrence, for such misfortunes are not often mentioned in the legends. Fortunately a tipi, unlike a permanent residence, can be taken down and loaded on a travois in a matter of minutes. In a few hours it can be many miles away in a safe location.

Life in a winter camp set up in a sheltered bend of the river was pleasant. The men conducted patrols, hunted, herded their horses, and generally participated in games of various kinds. Only occasionally did they go in the cold season on raiding expeditions to the camps of their enemies, for snow made it difficult to travel and very hard to stay hidden, while even the most inexperienced child could read tracks in snow. Much time was spent by the men just loafing, story-telling, and gambling, especially on the stick game, which involved moving one marked and one plain object swiftly from hand to hand, then challenging the opponent to guess which was which. Those entrusted with the instruction and education of boys in preparation for their becoming warriors were occupied in teaching the many spiritual rituals and the use of arms. It was a time for making weapons, and practising their use. Besides making their own feather head-dresses and clothing, the men also braided their rawhide ropes, and carved and decorated their medicine pipes.

The women, by contrast, were always busy in a winter camp sewing their clothing, tipi covers, and moccasins for all, and embroidering their various garments with dyed porcupine quills or bone beads. This was meticulous, time-consuming work, often conducted by several women coming together around the fireplace of a tipi, where they sat on robes against willow back-rests and gossiped as they worked and periodically attended to infants resting in cradle boards.

Much of the time, the women were out gathering wood and carrying water. Water was transported and stored in stomach bags taken from buffalo, elk, and deer. Buffalo paunches made the most durable containers. The bladders of these animals were also used as containers for various uses, and for toys resembling painted balloons.

Pemmican, which was made of dried meat and berries pounded together with tallow, was stored in rawhide bags around the outer wall of the tipi behind the draft curtain. Other rawhide bags and boxes containing jerky, herbs, dried roots, berries, and articles of clothing were stored in the same way. Fresh meat was hung from a pole rack outside the tipi, high enough to be out of reach of dogs, and the women spent much of their time preparing and cooking food.

The menu for every meal largely consisted of meat, with various other dishes such as meat broth and berry soup added. The early camps of the Blackfoot did their cooking either by broiling over hot coals, or by boiling the meat in crude clay pots or in a hollowed-out section of cottonwood log. Meat and whatever other ingredients were available were mixed with water in the log or the clay pot and then very hot rocks were dropped into the mix as needed to keep it boiling until cooked. Meals were not necessarily prepared at a given time during the day, but something was generally simmering by the fire. If a hunter came home tired and hungry, he was given something to eat and a change of clothing and moccasins by the women of his lodge. The women were proud of their lodge furnishings and kept them neat and comfortable. A well-kept tipi was a happy winter abode for a family.

On good days when the weather allowed, the children would take their sleighs made of buffalo ribs and have a joyous time sliding down a neighbouring steep slope. They would also go to the frozen surface of the nearby river and spin tops carved from wood, which they flung off a string wound around it. Sometimes they competed to see who could make a top spin the longest time and sometimes they threw the top at a mark. A specially carved long stick with a curved end like a sleigh runner was a favourite plaything, called a snow snake. It was flung to glide on the slippery surface and, as in a javelin-throwing contest, it was the distance that counted.

They were, in the old days in the wilds, a very strong and healthy people, powerful children of the outdoors. Their teeth were good because of the kind of food they ate. They did suffer from common colds, but organic problems such as heart disease and other diseases of the main organs were minimal.

Not very much can be written about their remedies or what their medicine men and women used in their treatments because it has always been held sacred, something passed down through the generations by word of mouth. Some of us do know, however, that the depth of their learning is profound, and even though most of us do not have the opportunity to understand it because we do not have the spiritual capacity, this does not mean that it is all superstition, with no real power of healing. They were great healers, and many of them still are. Just because medical science does not recognize the worth of their system does not mean it is worthless; it only means that we need broader and deeper vision. Indian medicine has its limitations, just as our medicine has, but that does not detract from its successes or lessen its possibilities.

They were great believers in training to toughen the body as well, as we will see now, as we take a look at a winter camp pitched in a bend of the Oldman, cleverly placed on a flat sheltered to the south and west by a grove of big old cottonwoods, with thickets of willows growing among them here and there. It is dawn on a crystal-clear winter morning with fresh snow on the ground and on the branches of the trees, and the temperature is well below zero. The people are stirring, and smoke columns rise from the tipis in the still air as wood is put on the banked fires, stirring them into flame. The horse herd is bunched up on the bluffs of the valley slopes to the north, a few of them feeding but most of them standing humped up in the cold waiting for the sun. The river skirting the cottonwoods behind the camp is frozen over and silent under its winter blanket of ice and snow.

Out of one of the lodges comes an old man wearing a buffalo-hide robe tied around the waist with a strip of buckskin, his long grey braids framing a weather-wrinkled face that has seen many winters. He is tall, though his shoulders are bowed, but he strides purposefully through the trees toward the river, his moccasins stirring little puffs of the new snow at every step.

When he comes to the river, he walks out on the ice to a place where there is a slight depression in the snow. Taking a small stone axe from under his belt, he begins chipping at the ice, clearing it from a long, narrow hole that has frozen over during the night. As he breaks it, he pushes the pieces under the ice, where they are carried away by the fast-running current. When he is finished, he has cleared a hole about thirty feet long and three feet wide. The water is about knee-deep and the gravel bottom is clearly visible.

As he straightens up, his austere old face softens and his mouth curls in a slight smile as he nods and gives a soft word of greeting to a young warrior and two boys, one about ten and the other a couple of years younger. They are wearing buckskin leggings and moccasins, and each has a robe slung around the shoulders with the hair side against their bodies. Kicking away the snow, they strip quickly; then, leaving their clothing on the bare ice, the two boys step toward the water. The oldest steps unhesitatingly into it, but the youngest pauses, hugging himself as he looks down and shivers. Before he can move, the warrior steps forward, puts a foot against his buttocks, and gives him a shove that propels him into the water with a splash. With a great gasp he catches his balance and begins to bathe, while his mentor steps in beside him and immerses his entire body before sitting up and beginning to scrub himself vigorously. The bath is short but it is thorough, and when it is through, they dress themselves quickly and head out on a long trot in the direction of the tents. On the way they pass other men and boys on their way to their morning bath – something all the men and boys over five years old do as a daily ritual. It is part of their training – a toughening exercise to make them able to endure exposure to any weather. Only the old men are excused in this kind of weather, for their joints and muscles are stiffening, and when it comes to being tough, they have nothing to prove.

As the morning bathing goes on, the sun comes up, painting the slopes in pink, and frost crystals glitter everywhere among the trees. There is laughter as two young boys chase a pup dragging a fragment of hide, their breath showing in puffs of steam as they run. Now people are visible everywhere among the lodges. It is a scene

that is alive and utterly beautiful as they move about in the early
sun.

They were very clean people, these early Blackfoot, much cleaner,
for instance, than their contemporaries in unwashed Europe. Men
and women bathed every day, the women in the tipis during cold
weather. In summer, they too took to the river, but at a different
time from the men. If a youngster became unduly obstreperous, he
might be punished by being taken to the river and pushed in, clothing and all, but the Blackfoot never struck their children.

While they were always spiritually close to the rivers, particularly
the Oldman, they never used them as a way to travel by either canoe
or bull-boat. The latter was a round boat made of buffalo hide
stretched over a willow frame, which the Sioux, Mandan, and other
Plains tribes used to cross big rivers like the Missouri and the
Yellowstone to the south. The Blackfoot people did not try to cross
the rivers until they were well past full flood. In the old dog days
they waded the shallow crossings pushing crude rafts that carried
their belongings. If they came to a channel too deep to wade, they
clung to the rafts and propelled them by kicking their feet. After
they got horses, they would take to swimming water, either hanging on to the side of the mount or being towed along grasping the
swimming horse's tail.

In spite of their close proximity to rivers over countless generations, it is notable that very few of the Blackfoot learned to swim,
just as few learned to fish, or to eat the day's catch. One reason for
their reticence no doubt lay in their belief that a water monster lived
in the Oldman, a legend that may have originated and been sus-
tained when they saw great black sturgeon swimming in it. These
big fish sometimes reached a length of fourteen feet and attained a
weight of five hundred pounds or more; they were not uncommon
in the old days as they ran up the Saskatchewan and its larger tributaries from Lake Winnipeg.

One legend tells of a time when two Sarcee warriors were coming
north heading for their camp. They were tired and very hungry

when they came to the Oldman and found a "water monster" lying stranded and dead on a sandbar. In spite of dire warnings from his partner, one warrior got off his horse, cut a piece of flesh off the monster, and ate it.

After they had travelled some distance further toward the Bow, this man complained of feeling very strange, and he told his partner that he was sure he was turning into a water monster. He instructed him that when they got to the Bow, he was to throw him in and leave him. This was done—and from that time on, the Blackfoot people believed that the Bow was also occupied by a water monster.

Despite their concerns about the water monsters or the more prevalent bad spirits who lived in the water, the warriors often broke young horses by leading them into hip-deep muddy backwaters and sloughs. Then, getting on their backs, they would ride them out. Dismounting before the horse could get onto firm footing and buck them off, they would repeat the process until the horse was too tired to buck, and they could ride it anywhere. Less usefully, but for the sheer fun and daring of it, young braves often rode their horses into the Oldman on hot summer days for a swim. Sometimes riding them, sometimes hanging onto the mane or the tail, they would steer them by splashing water at their heads from one side or the other with a free hand.

In those early days the flats and bluffs by the Oldman were often black with buffalo as far as the eye could see. Thousands of them were in sight, but that was only a small part of the millions wandering the plains between Lake Winnipeg, the Mississippi, and the Rocky Mountains. It was one of the grandest displays that nature has ever conceived—a magnificent example of an animal completely adapted to its environment, through which the Indian wandered totally in tune with it.

Of all the other animals they knew, the grizzly bear was perhaps the one they revered above all others. The plains grizzly was very numerous in those days, ranging from Lake Winnipeg and the Mississippi River to the shores of the Pacific, and from Mexico north to the edge of the Arctic Ocean. To the Peigans it was endowed with much power, both muscular and spiritual. Sometimes a small group of young braves out to prove their courage and to make names for themselves would tangle with one of the big animals armed only with lances. Running up to it they would provoke a charge, and while one fled, the others would harass the bear until it turned to chase them.

It was no kind of game to be played by any but the bravest and fleetest of foot. Back and forth they raced, dodging the furious animal until finally it was so weakened by wounds that they could kill it at leisure. Nor was the game always one-sided, for the grizzly's raking claws often left deep wounds and sometimes even killed. One slip or misstep was all it took for a warrior to be severely wounded or wiped out. But when they came home with the claws, there was much celebration. They never kept the hide, for nobody would touch it; it was taboo, although a warrior could proudly wear a claw necklace.

It was in winter that they hunted buffalo for their robes, which were prime between November and February, with thick wool and hair. From a big winter camp, the hunters would range forth on their hunting horses for miles in every direction, and cold weather did not stop them. They wore winter moccasins made from cow-buffalo skin with the hair side in, leggings made of the same stuff, a buckskin shirt, a fur cap, and a pair of gloves. They skinned their kills bare-handed in weather so cold that the hide froze solid as soon as it was taken off the carcass. Pack-trains of horses tended by the women went to a killing-ground to load up with meat. The hunters often piled all the meat they could on their horses, threw a robe over it, and came into camp sitting on top of the load. The snow was splotched with blood for miles, the horses were stained with it, and the people, men and women alike, were smeared with it from head to foot.

Once in a while over long intervals of a hunter's life news would come into camp of the sighting of an albino buffalo. Nothing could be more exciting to the hunters, for they believed that the white buffalo, with its pink eyes, hoofs, and horns, was a sacred animal. But if such a rare buffalo was not killed on the first sighting, it was generally very difficult to relocate it on prairies black with thousands of them for miles, particularly against a snowy background.

No effort would be spared in such a case, however, and often such a hunt involving many hunters would go on for days. When the albino was killed, its robe was very carefully removed from the carcass, including the scalp, horns, and hoofs. The meat was never taken but left for the wolves, while the robe was carried to camp and carefully dressed and tanned. It was almost inevitably given to the Sun at the next sun-dance ceremony the following summer with many prayers.

5   *The Stoneys*

The Blackfoot tribe went up the Oldman into the valley past the Gap only rarely, and then it was only to gather tipi poles from the lodgepole pine of the mountains. They did not go to hunt or to camp for any protracted period of time, for they were hunters of the plains and did not know how to hunt mountain animals on the high, steep slopes. They were also somewhat awed by mountains, and while they travelled through them on raids into the Kutenai country to the west, they never felt at home in them.

This was the land of the Stoneys. The mountains from up on the headwaters of the Athabasca River near Jasper south to the American border was the hunting country of the Stoney tribe, and they were a most important part of the Indian culture on the headwaters of the Oldman.

Before the horse came to the northern plains, the Stoneys had split off from the Assiniboine people in Manitoba far to the east. They were part of the great Sioux Nation, who spoke the language of the Nakota branch of these people. When they set out on the trek west across the northern plains and parklands, they were harried by the Ojibway, Crees, and Blackfoot, and their fighting strategy was somewhat limited by the flatter ground, for they were hill people.

Consequently they kept moving, and when they reached some broken country not far west of where Edmonton is now located, a large party of Sarcee warriors of the Blackfoot people attacked them. It was a mistake, for here the Stoneys were in rough ground and they out-manoeuvred the Sarcees and gave them a sound beating in a battle that was bloody and ruthless. When the surviving Sarcee warriors limped back and reported on it, they described these enemies as being stony-hearted. And thus, legend has it, they earned their name.

When they came to the mountains west of the scene of this great battle, they looked up at the towering peaks of the Rockies, which made those of their old hunting-grounds look like gopher mounds by comparison, and liked what they saw. Soon their hunting country ranged far and wide in the foothills and mountains of southwest Alberta, including the upper valleys of the Oldman River. They hunted the buffalo along the western rim of the plains and foothills east of the Continental Divide. In the mountains they also preyed on the bighorn sheep, mountain goats, deer, elk, moose, and bear west as far as the Kutenai, Shushwap, and Flathead country.

They were great climbers and wore special climbing moccasins soled with the thick neck and rump skin of male mountain goats. These high-climbing animals have short, black curving horns as sharp as daggers and are fierce fighters in the mating season, and somewhat truculent with each other at any time. For protection they have developed skin on their necks and rumps an inch thick, from which the Stoneys made buckskin, tough and spongy, that would cling to the rocks like rubber.

When it came to using steep terrain for fighting and hunting, the Stoneys were great strategists. When hunting, they would deploy hunters in rock blinds located on the saddles and passes at the head of a canyon. When all was ready, the women, old men, dogs, and youngsters would drive the valley from below with much yelling, yapping, and banging of sticks on the trees. Naturally the animals headed for high ground over familiar trails and when they passed the hidden hunters they were ambushed and killed. Some of the remnants of these old blinds are still visible.

Unlike the Blackfoot people, they ate fish, and were avid fishermen. They were experts with snares and took fish in the clear pools by fashioning a noose made of braided strands of sinew, heavily greased, which they fastened to the end of a long, slim pole. Standing on a ledge over the water or on a log-jam, they would slip the end of the pole into the water and with great skill manoeuvre the noose over the head of a trout or a whitefish. Then they would jerk it tight behind the gills and flip the catch out on shore. Such fish were split, sun-dried, and smoked to preserve them for winter use.

With the help of a dog, the women and children hunted grouse in the same fashion. The dog jumped the birds up into the trees, where they perched, stretching their necks as they watched the animal yapping and jumping about below. While their attention was thus diverted, the hunter lifted the pole and very carefully slipped the noose over the bird's head. A quick jerk decapitated it and another bird was ready for a tasty stew or for grilling over a bed of coals. The youngsters also snared ground squirrels in the same way by placing the noose around the entrance of a den and waiting for the animal to stick its head up for a look around before coming out to feed.

We white-skinned young hunters and gatherers who came later adopted these tricks from our brown-skinned brothers to take fish, birds, and small animals. We substituted brass wire for our nooses and they were very effective. With a little practice, you could take enough fish to make a meal for a whole family in a few minutes out of a pool with a school of whitefish and trout lining its bottom. We never went anywhere in the mountains without a length of brass wire, which not only provided a way of getting food in an emergency but was also handy for mending almost anything that needed it. As a matter of fact, I still carry brass wire if I am travelling by horse or on foot in the mountains, as a part of my survival gear.

Like all the Indians of the west, the Stoneys were a highly spiritual people, who hunted only out of need – for food and for the various parts of animals that they used every day.

They were migratory people travelling through and living close to the mountains, and, unlike the Plains Indians, they had three kinds of dwellings – seasonal, portable, and permanent. In June, when the sap was up, they peeled the bark off standing spruce trees in large slabs; overlapping one another, these slabs were used to cover lodge poles set up in a cone, the same as the tipi. For their portable tipis they used the regular skin covers, made from the hides of buffalo, moose, and elk.

Their permanent shelters, to withstand the bitter winters of the mountains, were pole-and-moss dwellings of two kinds. One was a tipi about ten feet across at the base and from twelve to sixteen feet high. The poles were set in circular tipi style, but with the straight poles wedged very close together, with green moss pushed in tight between the poles. This was overlapped with another layer of poles also chinked with moss to form a double layer. The other type of permanent dwelling was constructed in rectangular shape about twelve feet wide, fourteen feet high, and twenty feet long, with a gable roof. This, too, was of double pole-and-moss construction. Well insulated, these dwellings were cool in summer and warm in winter. They were located all over their hunting-grounds, and belonged to nobody, but were used by all members of the tribe who needed them while hunting or on a journey.

In those prehistory times the Stoneys and all other Indians were basically very healthy and active. Scientists tell us that they did not suffer from heart disease to any extent, and cancerous growths were practically unknown, while their diet of meat and wild berries and roots – not to mention the absence of refined sugar – gave them good sound teeth. Their medicine men, who had a profound knowledge of the relationship between the body, the mind, and the spirit, were great healers. The counselling skills of modern-day psychiatrists were well known in their cultures. They did not deal with parts of people but with the whole person. Just as they had no jails, or special dwellings for old people not considered useful, or any asylums for the insane, they had no fear of death, nor any belief in hell. They believed that a person's spirit went to dwell in a very beautiful and wonderful spirit world when they died. Atheism was unknown among them – they had no word for it in their language, nor any knowledge of it.

Like most mountain people, they had courage and physical strength unsurpassed by any, and their many legends tell of bravery while fighting with their enemies. Many of the stories tell of Stoneys able to change themselves into animals. One particular legend tells of how Wolf-Come-Into-View was approached by a spirit in wolf guise, who gave him a gift, which he could use to get himself out of difficult situations.

On one occasion, he was out among the high hills overlooking the Oldman, scouting for buffalo in the valley below, when he spotted some enemy Blackfoot who were also hunting. They saw him before he could hide, and, whooping in triumph, proceeded to come after him. He ran into some bushes close by and called on his wolf spirit to save him.

The enemy warriors scoured the brush attempting to find him, with no success. Finally one of the Blackfoot warriors pointed and called, "Look over there." The others turned to see a wolf loping away over the skyline on top of a hill. The enemy leader told his men, "Do not bother. That man has turned into a wolf. He must be spiritually gifted, and a great warrior."

So, from that time on, Wolf-Come-Into-View was highly respected by all enemy warriors.

The Stoneys lived close to the mountains and thought of them as sacred. They were the monuments of nature, a constant reminder of the power of the Great Spirit. Warmed by the sun, caressed by the winds, and blanketed in white by the storms of winter, they were a most powerful part of the natural world. To be sure, the mountains could be dangerous and sometimes people were killed by an avalanche, or injured in a fall while climbing. At times the lightning of summer thunderstorms set fires that raged down the valleys, burning everything and leaving the trees blackened and dead in their wake. But always the heat of such fires caused the accumulated seeds of the lodgepole pine to sprout. These grew slim and tall among the deadfall timber of the burn slowly rotting on the ground, and in time provided an abundance of poles for constructing lodges.

Old people and the sick made journeys up to the hot springs on the Bow River, where they bathed and soaked themselves in the hot water to cleanse themselves and regained their health and vigour. These medicine baths were a regular practice of the Stoneys, until after the white man came and created Banff, Kootenay, and Jasper National Parks. Then, to our shame, they were barred from the hot springs, which were developed and used exclusively by white tourists who knew nothing and cared even less about the ritualistic healing practices of these Indians.

When the Stoneys got horses and became skilful in using them for hunting, packing, and pulling travois, they, like all the western Indians, found life much easier. I remember as a small boy seeing the tracks and trails used by their hunting parties on the edge of the mountains some sixty years ago.

Once, as a young man guiding some guests into the mountains, I was looking for our horses up on the headwaters of the Oldman River. It was before sun-up on a cold, frosty October morning when I found a bunch of Indian horses feeding on a meadow in a twisted little valley. Riding on to find our bunch, I came upon a very old man walking. He did not speak much English and I knew no words of Stoney, but by use of sign language and by drawing a map and some pictures in the dust of the trail, it was not long before we understood each other. I had found his horses and he had found mine.

I went on and soon came to a Stoney camp, a hunting party led by a big strong Indian known as King Bear's Paw, son of the Stoney chief Bear's Paw. They had meat hung up and a fresh bear hide laced into a pole frame. A woman was busy scraping the fat off the bear hide, another was working with a deer hide, and there were several black-eyed youngsters standing around looking at me very solemnly. King Bear's Paw, who spoke good English, told me with much gesturing and enthusiasm how his dogs had fought with the bear and then chased it up a tree, where he had shot it.

When I had gathered my horses and was driving them back toward our camp, I met the old man riding a pony bareback and herding his horses up the trail. He was puffing away happily on a huge cigar one of our guests had given him at our camp, and carrying a roll of toilet-paper – a somewhat droll gift from the same source. He also had a bag of tea in one of his pockets that Bert Riggall, the head guide, had given him.

Pointing to the roll of toilet-paper, I asked with a smile, "What's that for?" The old Indian grinned from ear to ear and said, "Give'm squaw. Buck use'm stick!"

One time I was sitting visiting with Chief John Snow of the Stoney tribe telling stories when the question of how Indians came to be called Indians came up. I commented that when Columbus came to North America, he thought he had found India; consequently he called the natives he encountered Indians in his logbook, and the name stuck. John quietly digested this bit of historic information for a while, then his eyes gave away his humour as he said, "Good thing he wasn't looking for Turkey!"

John Snow is a highly educated man, an ordained minister of the United Church, who presided over a church at Morley, Alberta, for a number of years before being elected as chief of the tribe. Disillusioned by Christianity, he has gone back to his native religion. He is the author of the book *These Mountains Are Our Sacred Places*, one of the finest books ever written on the history of native people and a very thorough account of the Stoney tribe, past and present.

The Oldman River knew his people and their ways well. Some of the old trails they made along the steep slopes and over the passes of the Rockies drained by it are still visible, though in places there are big trees growing on them at least seventy-five years old.

6 *First Contact*

The Mountain and Plains Indians, of which the Blackfoot people were a part, had brought the Stone Age to its highest degree of cultural development. The acquisition of horses had left them with time to think, and to enjoy the long sweep of the hills and prairies. They did not live in the past but only looked back over it, making use of the many things that it had taught them since the very dim era of the ice, when, the old legends reminded them, they had hunted huge hairy beasts with tremendously long teeth, so big that it took only one to feed a campful of people for a long time.

They could camp beside and sing about their holy river that was born in the mountains and still carried the cold feel of the icy womb from which it sprang. Indeed, in summer the Stoneys could climb the ridge flanking the grasslands and hills north of the trail through the Gap. Walking along the ridge, looking west to the great wall of peaks that cleared the sky, they could almost see where the river started from the ground. They could walk on to the north and climb over the rounded limestone dome of Hailstone Butte, down through a deep saddle, and then up again onto the rim of Flattop Mountain, a high, grassy plateau. Down off the rim on its northern side, they may have come upon a cave that was still choked with old prehistoric ice unmelted over the ages of time, as it still is today. When they touched the water slowly dripping off the ice, it no doubt made their skins crawl and they got out into the sun as quickly as possible, realizing why their river born of these mountains was so cold.

Their horses allowed them to range widely from camps around the river. Now when a hunter climbed a hill and looked east toward a herd on the horizon, it did not seem so far away, even in winter, when meat was needed. Mounted on their trained buffalo runners the men could ride out to a distant herd and kill enough to keep the camp for weeks. In war, too, the tempo was stepped up, for the fighters were now fleet-footed cavalry able to move great distances in a short time and to manoeuvre skilfully and fast on a battlefield.

It was not only the hunters and warriors who benefited, for their women did not have to work so hard, their babies were better fed and healthier, and the old people, always revered for their knowledge and experience, had a much easier time in the evening of their lives.

It was truly the golden age of the plains people, a democracy of deep communal strength in which there were rich and poor, but there was nobody who went hungry or unsheltered. The Blackfoot were one of the strongest tribes, but because the various leaders of the family bands within the tribe were so independent and proud, inter-tribal politics were ponderous and slow. It never occurred to them to join with such enemies as the Sioux, Crows, Kutenais, and Crees to form a grand alliance. Revenge for past incidents of war was too strong an influence, and raiding for enemy horses was too exciting a game to be put aside for the sake of greater strength.

Just the same, this was a budding new civilization in North America. All it needed to bloom was the appearance of a strong man of sufficient political intelligence, ambition, and charisma to bring it to fruition. If the horse Indians of the great plains had ever united, they might have become a great power. But fate was pulling them in another direction.

From around the time that they acquired horses, the Blackfoot people were probably aware of the intrusion of white men, for the Spanish conquistadors had been firmly established in Mexico for almost two centuries, and from there had taken expeditions far afield. No doubt stories were told in the Blackfoot tipis pitched along the Oldman River of these strange men with pallid skins and hair on their faces, who wore hard shirts that could stop an arrow and rode big "medicine dogs". Following 1670, when the Hudson's Bay Company built its first trading-post on the shores of Hudson Bay, far to the northeast, they had been aware of white men living there, for the Crees and Assiniboines had acquired some wondrous things, such as brass kettles, iron axes and knives, and colourful glass beads, as well as marvellous fire sticks that belched fire and smoke and threw a smooth stone farther than the flight of an arrow. Some of these strange objects may have even filtered through to them through inter-tribal trade or war.

Then, one summer day in 1754, news came to a big camp of Peigans pitched on the rolling prairie about halfway between the Red Deer and Bow rivers that a strange white man was coming with a small party of Crees. He was Anthony Henday from Fort York on Hudson Bay, and he had made his way by canoe to Lake Winnipeg and then up the Saskatchewan, probably to Battle River. When the water became too shallow to navigate, he had left his canoes and struck out on foot heading west, on the look-out for the Indians who inhabited this great prairie country to try to persuade them to come east to the post and trade their furs.

Henday later recorded how impressed he was to come within sight of this camp of about two hundred tipis pitched in two long lines, with the far end blocked by a big tipi with two doors. As he marched into the lane between the tents leading his party, his naval uniform of blue wool cloth, trimmed with gold braid and brass buttons, and his freshly polished boots caused the Peigans standing in front of their tipis to cover their mouths with their hands in wonder. He was duly ushered into the big tent, where he was greeted by the chief and his council of band leaders. Assisted by a Cree who had spent some time with the Peigans and knew their language as well as some English, he proceeded to give presents of tobacco, beads, and sundry other items and was welcomed with speeches, food, and genuine hospitality. He was the first white man the Peigans had ever seen and no doubt generated considerable awe and excitement among them, though their faces never betrayed it.

There was the usual round of pipe-smoking and talk, and finally Henday invited the chief to send some of his people down the big river and thence to Fort York to trade. With great dignity and considerable oratorical skill, the chief told him that the Blackfoot lived a long way from the white man's camp; it would be a very hard and dangerous journey for them, for they rode horses, had no boats, and did not know how to use them. They would likely starve before they got back from that land of big rivers, forests, and rocks. He pointed out that his people had everything they needed here, for the Old Man was good to them and gave them the buffalo and many other things.

Looking around him at the richly decorated clothes and sleeping-robes, the spacious painted tipis, the powerfully built people and their numerous horses, Henday no doubt realized that the chief had a strong argument. It was a very long journey to Fort York, as he knew at first hand, through a country with nothing like the richness of wild animals seen every day on these plains of grass, but plagued with clouds of mosquitoes and blackflies. He thought of these people as savages, but their pride and self-sufficiency could not be denied. In due course he left with all the furs he could carry, a story to tell the chief factor at Fort York, and the memory of a glimpse of shining mountains on the western horizon. He was the first white man to see the northern Rockies. As for the Peigans, they also had something new to talk about, and various articles to remind them of his visit.

The Europeans intruding into this vast wilderness had originally come searching for an ocean passage from the Atlantic to the

Pacific and the Orient; a shortcut to the silk, spices, and other riches of far-away India and China. Arctic ice and deadly cold had defeated the quest, but the fur trade offered a good excuse to push westward, following the dream of finding a navigable river road that would lead in the same direction. Consequently, white traders began to show up with greater frequency in the Blackfoot country, and from them the people of the plains acquired guns, and many other intriguing things, including rum and brandy.

Perhaps the first white man to live among the Peigans was John Munroe, a remarkable man of well-educated background born in Trois-Rivières, Quebec, in 1798. When he was only fifteen years of age, he persuaded his parents to allow him to go west with the Hudson's Bay Company. They agreed, and away he went with a brigade of canoes following the route to the head of the Great Lakes and then on to Lake Winnipeg, where the party spent the winter. After spring break-up, they proceeded west, and in July 1814 came to Edmonton House on the Saskatchewan River only two hundred miles from the foot of the Rockies.

The surrounding flats and meadows were covered with the tipis of a great gathering of Peigans waiting for the goods from the east to arrive, so that they could trade for the things they needed to see them through the following year. The white traders, however, were somewhat at a loss to communicate with them, for they had no interpreter. So the local factor detailed young Munroe to live and travel with the Peigans, learn their language, and see to it that they returned to the fort the following summer with their furs. No doubt the company knew that the American traders were pushing west following Lewis and Clark's trail and worried that the Blackfoot tribes to the south would go to them; John Munroe was to do everything possible to prevent it.

J.W. Schultz tells how Munroe soon found himself riding with the Peigan chiefs and medicine men at the front of a long procession involving about two hundred lodges, one thousand people, and a big horse herd. Near the end of the day, they came to a valley where a tree-lined stream wound through some big flats; the chiefs pulled off to the side to sit at the top of a hill and watch the procession pass into the valley, and wait for the women to put up the lodges. One of the medicine men took out a pipe, loaded it with tobacco, and then tried in vain to light it with flint and steel and a bit of punk. John Munroe asked for the pipe, took out his burning-glass (magnifying glass), focussed it on the tobacco to set it alight, and drew several puffs through the long stem.

Instantly there was a terrific hullabaloo among the watching Indians, who pressed forward yelling and swarming around him. Munroe was thoroughly frightened. When some mothers started to rub their babies against him, it finally dawned on him that his Peigan hosts thought that by holding his hand up to the sun (they had not seen the glass), he had called on the power of the Old Man to light the pipe. He was suddenly big medicine.

The head chief of the big band was Lone Walker, and when Munroe went to visit him at his lodge that evening, he was greeted by heavy growls on either side of the doorway, and saw two almost full-grown young grizzly bears threatening to jump on him. The chief spoke to them quietly and they immediately lay down, nose on paws, like two great dogs. It took Munroe some time to become accustomed to the bears; finally, though, he could come and go without being greeted with growls, but they never allowed him to touch them. Lone Walker, however, fed them and handled them. When they moved camp, the two grizzlies trailed his travois with the dogs, and at night they always slept as guards on each side of the door of his tipi. He kept them until the following spring, when one night they just walked away and were never seen again. Lone Walker looked far and wide for them for days, and was disconsolate over the loss of his pets.

The great procession of people, horses, and dogs went on southward, camping for a while on the Oldman, and then setting out again. During the season of the falling leaves they made a winter camp on the Pile of Rocks River, now known as the Sun.

One by one Munroe's garments wore out and he was given soft tanned deer and bighorn skins by Lone Walker's women to make more for himself. Soon he was clad from head to foot in leather shirt, leggings, breech-clout, and moccasins – a picturesque figure with his long fair hair rippling to his shoulders. He was about five feet seven inches tall, very quick and sure in his movements, with the air of a man of determination and courage, and had been given the Peigan name of Rising Wolf.

He was now living in Lone Walker's lodge, where he was greatly struck by the presence of a very lovely girl, three years younger than he, though a fully developed woman. By Peigan rules, they never spoke, although by now Rising Wolf was becoming fluent in the language. At every opportunity, as they sat across the lodge from each other, they shyly exchanged looks. Days, weeks, and months went by.

Then one evening a man came visiting and began to praise a certain young brave with whom Rising Wolf had often hunted and ridden. He told of his many virtues and his wealth, and went on to say that the young brave was presenting Lone Walker with thirty horses – and he wished to set up a lodge of his own with the chief's daughter, Ap'-ah-ki. Rising Wolf glanced at the girl, to find her looking at him. After a pause, Lone Walker praised the young man with much sincerity, but stated that, for all that, he could not give him his daughter.

Ap'-ah-ki's face now wore a smile and her eyes shone, but Rising Wolf was gloomy. What hope had he of getting the girl? He owned no horses, and received only twenty pounds a year in salary from the company. What chance did he have of even coming close to meeting such an offer? Time passed and he constantly racked his brains for a feasible plan, but none came.

Then one evening a couple of weeks later he met her on the trail carrying a bundle of firewood. They looked at each other in silence for a while, then Rising Wolf spoke her name. After an interlude, he told her that he was going to speak to her father, to which she readily agreed. When they came to him, hand in hand, the old chief smiled and quietly puffed his pipe.

"I have not thirty horses," said Rising Wolf, "not even one, but we love each other! I ask you to give her to me."

"Why did you think I refused thirty horses? I need a white man for a son-in-law. I need a counsellor. We are not blind. We waited for you to speak the word. There is nothing more to say, except: be good to her."

That very day a lodge was set up for them, complete with all furnishings and necessary equipment. Lone Walker instructed Rising Wolf to choose thirty horses from his herd. They were very happy, and stayed so happy that Rising Wolf never returned to his family back east. He and Ap'-ah-ki had a large family, and many of their descendants are still alive.

By the end of the eighteenth century, the Hudson's Bay Company was being challenged in the trading business by the North West Company under the management of an enterprising group of Scotsmen based in Montreal. Contracting with tough French Canadians for canoemen and traders, this company freighted many tons of goods in great canoes up the Ottawa from the St. Lawrence over a portage to the head of the French River and down to the Great Lakes. Then they followed the chain of lakes west to the far reaches of Lake Superior, where they built a huge double-walled fort which they called Grande Cache. From this staging-centre in the wilderness the trade goods were loaded into smaller canoes that could navigate the inland streams, and then they pressed on even farther to the west and north to search out the Indian camps and thus bring the trade to them on their hunting-grounds.

It was only when the trade slowed to a trickle at their posts that the officers of the Hudson's Bay Company stirred themselves to look westward. For a long time they had required the Indians to come to them. Now they realized that they were going to have to get out there toward the Rocky Mountains if they were to compete successfully. With some bitterness, they called the French traders who were outflanking them "bloody pedlars", but they took up the challenge, and the competition for furs was on with a vengeance. The Indians, no mean bargainers themselves, were not slow about playing one company against the other, although there were times when they were abused and cheated by both.

Among the major figures in this exploration of the western wilderness was the legendary Peter Pond, a Connecticut Yankee who established a post in the fabulously rich beaver country of the Athabasca for the North West Company. Energetic, bad-tempered, and subject to flaming fits of jealousy, Pond was suspected of committing two murders during his career, but they were never proved. Irascible he might have been, but he was dreamer enough to open up the Athabasca territory as early as 1778 and deserved his legendary status.

Another was Alexander Mackenzie, born in Scotland, who was indentured as an apprentice at the age of fifteen with the North West Company's head office in Montreal. In 1785, when he was twenty-one years old, he was dispatched to the Athabasca post to winter with Peter Pond. Perhaps Pond was mellowing, for he was unusually friendly and helpful to young Mackenzie, telling him of his discoveries and his ambitious plans. He had explored as far north as Great Slave Lake, and although he had not seen it, the Indians had told him of a big river running west from its outlet. He also believed that the Rocky Mountains came to an end at about latitude 62 degrees, and that therefore this great range would not interfere with the river's course toward the Pacific. Neither he nor Mackenzie apparently realized that Indians have a genius for kind-heartedly telling a white man what they think he would like to hear, regardless of truth.

Anyway, at break-up time in the spring of 1789, Mackenzie made his way north and after considerable difficulty with floating ice found the river, which was running west. He followed it, only to find that after a few miles it turned north. But he stuck with it day after day and finally arrived at its big delta, and the shore of the

Arctic Ocean. He knew this was not the Pacific, so he headed his canoes back upstream and again wintered with Pond. He had traversed one of the biggest rivers of the world – a river that was named after him, even if it was not of much use to the trade.

It whetted his appetite for more exploring, and in 1793 he embarked on a journey up the Peace River. Reaching its headwaters among towering mountains, he crossed the Great Divide and launched his birch-bark canoes down a big river through stretches of wild whitewater. But it was flowing south, not west, which worried him. He cached his canoes at the outlet of the Blackstone and proceeded on foot over the Coast Range and down the Bella Coola River to the coast. Obtaining a dugout canoe from the Bella Coola Indians, he set out to go by sea south toward the mouth of the Columbia, which had been discovered earlier by Captain Vancouver, who had taken a ship around the Horn in the Antarctic. But he had hardly started before he ran into trouble with the Bella Bella Indians and was forced to retreat. In nine years, Mackenzie had journeyed across from Montreal down to the mouth of the Mackenzie and then across the mountains to the Pacific. He was twelve years ahead of the Lewis and Clark expedition, which reached the Pacific at the mouth of the Columbia from St. Louis, Missouri, in 1805.

In 1792, Peter Fidler, map-maker and explorer for the Hudson's Bay Company, came south from an expedition in the Athabasca country along the front of the mountains. Meeting up with a big camp of Peigans, he wintered with them on the headwaters of the Oldman. He was the first white man to see the pile of prayer stones at the Gap, which was then about sixteen feet across and eight feet high. Over the next century, the number of white men passing through that country would number in the thousands. But for now, only a few of the hardiest explorers reached as far as the Rockies.

In 1805, the same year that Lewis and Clark reached the coast, Simon Fraser, another tough Nor'Wester, was dispatched westward up the Peace. He was convinced that Mackenzie had been following the Columbia when he branched off it to walk west to the Pacific, and he followed the mystery river south. The farther he went, the bigger and wilder it became, until he too cached his canoes and continued on foot down past the terrible rapids in its great canyon. Finally he acquired dugout canoes from the Indians and proceeded to its mouth. Having read Captain Vancouver's log of his exploration of the Columbia, he knew he too had followed the wrong river. He was also absolutely sure that this one was not a navigable trade route.

At the same time that Fraser was battling his way down the terrifying river that was to bear his name, another determined explorer was getting set to map the country on the vast and complicated headwaters of the Columbia. He was David Thompson, the famous map-maker, and of all the explorers of the vast mountain wilderness, this was one who always knew where he was at any point, for he was an expert with the sextant. Not very big as men stand today, he was rawhide tough, an athlete of the first order, and very experienced. Over a relatively short time between 1799 and 1805 he had mapped a big portion of the country all the way from the head of the Great Lakes west to the Rockies.

In the spring of 1807 he took an expedition from Rocky Mountain House up the North Saskatchewan over a pass that led him down to a big river flowing swiftly north. He did not recognize it, but he was looking at the Columbia. He thought it was the Kootenay. He proceeded to build a big canoe and headed upstream to duly arrive at a beautiful lake now known as Lake Windermere. At a spot upriver a mile or two, he built a fort which he called Kootenay House. Here he met the Kutenai Indians, whom he befriended and who accompanied him on further travels in the area. This friendship, and the trade that was supposed to spring from it, caused him more trouble than he expected – from the Peigans, who often came west over various passes from their home range on the Oldman to raid the Kutenais.

After Thompson had built another small post near Kootenay Falls, he rode back with the chief to Kootenay House, where he

found the Indian camp and his people greatly worried about a bunch
of Peigan warriors lurking about in the vicinity. The Peigans were
just as worried about him, for they did not wish their old enemies
the Kutenais to get guns. Winter weather eventually drove the
Peigans back east over the Rockies before any harm was done. But
they carried the news of Thompson's doings back with them to the
chiefs and council of the tribe, a fact that was to prove very trouble-
some to him.

A year later he was back mapping the country between the
Kootenay and the Flathead River, at the same time working out
in his mind a route to the Columbia. Certainly nobody in the fur
trade could accuse Thompson of laziness; if going hell-for-leather
was what it took, then hell-for-leather he went. The distances he
covered were stupendous, and mountains and rivers did not seem to
slow him up. The trade was good, for the Kutenais and Flatheads
wanted guns, and while the numbers he could give them were
limited by transport, they got enough to be much better able to
deal with their traditional enemies from across on the Oldman River
country, who normally had far more guns than they did. As it
happened, the Kutenais made the best bows and arrows in the west,
beautiful, powerful weapons fashioned from straightened strips of
bighorn ram horn backed with sinew and finally covered with rattle-
snake skin, all bonded together with glue. These could propel an
arrow an incredible distance and were highly prized – but they were
no match for the guns of the Peigan raiders.

In the summer of 1811, something happened that was to compli-
cate David Thompson's life. A war party of Peigans ran head-on
into a bunch of Flathead and Kutenai hunters heading east across
the mountains to hunt buffalo, and a fight erupted. The fierce
battle, with guns on both sides, went on until the Peigans ran out
of ammunition and were reduced to throwing rocks. Then it was a
hand-to-hand mix-up along the crest of a ridge until finally the
Peigans were forced to retreat, leaving sixteen dead warriors behind.
It was the first time they had been up against guns in the hands of

these enemies, and the defeat turned them bitter against Thompson's trade. They determined to stop any further trade reaching over the pass on the head of the North Saskatchewan, and proceeded to set up a blockade.

Of course Thompson, again coming west upriver toward Rocky Mountain House with four canoeloads of goods, had no way of knowing about this battle. At Fort Augustus, not far from where Edmonton now stands, he obtained a string of horses and proceeded toward the mountains with the loaded canoes following him.

At some point downriver from Rocky Mountain House, which was being managed by Alexander Henry, two of Thompson's hunters spotted a Peigan camp and reported back to their boss. He, being a very cautious man and thoroughly respectful of the Peigans, immediately took cover with the rest of the mounted party on top of a heavily timbered hill. In the meantime, his canoes went blithely past, thinking he was still ahead of them. When they got to Rocky Mountain House, Alexander Henry assumed that Thompson had sneaked past the Peigan encampment by the fort and was now upriver toward Kootenay Plains. When a party of Peigans came downriver with a horse belonging to Thompson, he was sure.

Then began a kind of charade that was anything but funny for the traders. Henry's problem was to get the loaded canoes on up to Thompson without being discovered. So he proceeded to get the whole Peigan camp dead drunk on brandy and laudanum; but just about the time the canoes were ready to leave, more Indians showed up. So Henry waited for another suitably dark night, and again got all the Indians drunk, while telling them some great lies about what the canoes were doing at the post. In the meantime, the water in the river dropped and the packs had to be split to lighten the canoes enough to float. At the expense of more liquor, he finally got the canoes away upstream.

Then one of Thompson's men showed up from downriver with the news that he was in hiding, and starving, because nobody dared fire a shot in hunting for food. Totally exasperated, Henry had no

choice but to send his clerk, much against his will, upriver to bring
back the canoes. When this was accomplished, he loaded a string of
horses and set off downstream looking for Thompson and found him
completely frustrated, discouraged, and very hungry.

Thompson decided not to get involved in this dangerous non-
sense again. He resolved to outflank the Peigans by going north
with his horses and then west up the Athabasca into what is now
Jasper Park. He pressed on up the path of the Whirlpool River all
the way to the first recorded crossing of the Athabasca Pass, which
led him over and down to the Big Bend of the Columbia River in
late December. It was a very tough, epic journey, too detailed to tell
about here, but it opened a new trail into the Columbia River
country. For years this was to be the main fur-trade route across the
Rockies.

It all goes to illustrate the enormous respect that the Canadian
traders had for the Blackfoot people, and while much of the fore-
going account of the spread of exploration and trade may seem ex-
traneous to the subject of the Oldman River, it all ties in with the
rapid changes affecting the culture of the people who camped along
its banks. The Blackfoot were being slowly but surely surrounded,
and the age-old free-ranging days on the plains were surely num-
bered now.

Farther south, American beaver-trappers were invading Blackfoot
hunting-grounds on the upper headwaters of the Missouri River.
These mountain men were a rough, wild lot, some of them working
for the big New York- and St. Louis-based trading companies,
while others were independent fur-trappers who combed the creeks
for beaver pelts. Every summer, at a pre-arranged site, they all met
the traders' supply trains of horses and mules at a big rendezvous for
trade and the sale of their skins. When the Blackfoot were first invited to participate, they accepted the invitation. But, more by
accident than by design, a battle broke out that resulted in many
casualties among the Blackfoot, including some women and child-

ren. From that time on, they were implacable enemies of the American trappers.

By contrast, they maintained good relations, by and large, with the Canadian traders who exchanged furs for the guns and powder the Blackfoot now needed. With the rivalry between the Nor'-Westers and the Bay at an end, and the companies amalgamated under the Hudson's Bay Company flag, the trade steadied in a concerted push westward.

7 *The Dawn of a New Day*

The tempo of change was speeding up. To the south of the Oldman country, more and more white immigrants began showing up. Big wagon trains of American settlers heading for Oregon started travelling a trail up the Yellowstone River toward a pass over the divide there. These people were tough, enterprising, and determined to reach the promised land in the rich valleys over toward the coast. Occasionally raiding-parties of the Blackfoot attacked them, with heavy losses on both sides.

One party of farmers from Pennsylvania, Germans saddled with the "Pennsylvania Dutch" name, split off from a wagon train after an unfortunate disagreement, and headed north. Somehow they got through into the very heart of the Blackfoot country before their luck ran out. At a spot several miles west of the upper forks of the Oldman River, a Peigan war party hit them. In a scene associated by most Canadian readers only with Hollywood movies, not with real episodes from their own history, the settlers circled their wagons on top of a butte and a fierce fight ensued. But there were too many mounted Indians and the entire party of settlers was wiped out. Within living memory it was possible to pick up objects remaining from this battle on a lonely hilltop.

But other white inroads were more successful, and more deadly. Once, a party of raiding Crees were out after horses down along the Missouri River somewhere below Great Falls when they came upon a Sioux camp. Some of the Cree warriors penetrated right in among the tipis, eager to count coup by stealing some prized horses and whatever else they could find. They were surprised to meet with little resistance. Too late, they learned there was sickness in that camp, and when these warriors got back with whatever plunder they managed to pick up, one or two of them became very ill with a high fever that did not react to any of the traditional medicines of their people. It was smallpox, the dreaded disease of the white man, and it went through the people exposed to it like a prairie fire, for the Indians were particularly vulnerable to it and had no knowledge of its viral propensities or treatment. In a very short time all the Plains tribes were infected, and their numbers reduced to a mere fraction.

The Blackfoot thought that their Old Man had abandoned them. Whole camps were deserted, the standing tipis left flapping in the wind with dead bodies in them and around them. Never again would the people recover their old power.

No longer did the buffalo number in millions, for the hide-hunters were rapidly wiping them out, leaving the meat to rot in thousands of piles across the prairies. And as the buffalo herds dwindled, more white settlers came in, restricting their range even further. Following the American civil war, big cattle herds from Texas were moved north, fattening on the rich grass as they went, before being shipped east on a railroad that was being pushed west through Kansas.

Within a few years—a few grains of sand in the hourglass of time—the Great Plains of North America had been virtually emptied of one of the greatest herds of animals the world has ever seen. The prairie bison, numbering somewhere between sixty and a hundred million, commonly called buffalo by all, had virtually disappeared. So had the plains grizzly. Numbers of elk, deer, and prairie antelope were also at a low ebb, for both Indian and white hunters turned to them for meat when the buffalo disappeared. What had been a country that produced as many protein units of food per square mile as perhaps anywhere in recent history was now virtually empty. And the Plains Indians, the proud People of the Buffalo, were lost, stricken by the decimation of smallpox, and even denied the consolation of their religion.

When the first missionaries came to the prairies, the Blackfoot people, like all the native tribes, were torn between their traditional beliefs and Christianity. They had lived over thousands of years within the deeply spiritual world of nature, where all things related directly to their lives. Yet the doctrines of Christianity and the story of Christ's life were attractive to them, for they had come to view the white man as a symbol of great power through their acquisition of many things he offered them in trade, on which they had come to depend. The white man's medicine was strong – so powerful that they found themselves looking on Christianity as a way to overcome the obvious disparities between the races.

When smallpox and measles decimated their numbers and the buffalo began to disappear, most of them felt that the friendly spirits of the land and sky, with which they had lived so long, had abandoned them. In spite of the old medicine men, who fiercely and ceaselessly worked against the missionaries' influence, more and more of them adopted the new religion, assuming the role of born sinners doomed to the fires of hell unless they begged forgiveness of God and paid their tithes. As youngsters, they had been trained as hunters to leave bits of their kill for the spirits, to give away most of the meat and keep only a small portion for themselves. Now, as Christians, they were required to give one-tenth to the church, and had to keep the rest. There were wise men amongst them who questioned this; they questioned it even more as they watched their own representatives of government, the agents, stealing from them on the reservations, while the people starved for lack of adequate rations. Those Indians who had come to own cattle or even to farm grain could not sell an animal or a bushel of wheat or oats without the agent's permission, and the price was too often less than the market level, the difference being split between the agent and the buyer.

Once, short years ago, they had been a proud, strong, and totally self-sufficient people on the plains. Now, within the confines of the reservations, they became vassals of the Queen in far-off Britain across the big water – second-class citizens, completely at the mercy of the largely ignorant and uncaring bureaucrats of the Indian Department in Ottawa. Those proud old warriors who had known the fine, free days of buffalo-hunting and raiding for horses found the comparisons very sad indeed, and were ashamed.

Meanwhile their holy river, lovely and serene as always, saw the changes, but did not pause on its wild, free journey from the shining mountains to the distant ocean. The river never changed. Neither did the slopes and folds of the hills overlooking it, although in time they were scarred here and there by railroad grades and by the ruts left by wagons now even used by the Indians, though the old three-track trails of the travois were still visible in many places. Here and there on the reserves the old bleached centre poles of the traditional sun-dance lodges still stood in mute testimony to a profoundly meaningful old ceremony no longer allowed by the new regulations. It was a travesty of justice in a country proudly claiming that its citizens enjoyed freedom of religion. The regulations were later repealed, but not before they had served to reduce the inherent self-esteem of a proud race.

The history of the Plains Indians is not without its chroniclers. At Milk River, where it flows past to the north of the Sweetgrass Hills just a few miles east of the border town of Coutts, is a unique area known as Writing-on-Stone. Here, in the middle of the gently sloping grasslands of the surrounding prairie, the scenery is a total contrast of oddly shaped columns of sandstone, hoodoos, and sheer cliffs of soft grey capped by rust-brown slabs of harder rock. James Doty was the first white man to see this place in 1855 and he describes the cliffs: "They are worn by the action of weather into a thousand fantastic shapes, presenting in places smooth perpendicular surfaces covered by crude hieroglyphics and representations of men, horses, guns, bows, shields, etc. in the usual Indian style."

There are two kinds of these figures – some were carefully carved, while others were scratched and painted with red ochre. It is thought that at least some of this early art, apparently carved before the arrival of the horse, was the work of the Shoshoni Indians, who supposedly came north into the country of the Oldman about 1300. The art of this era shows warriors with shields big enough to cover them as they fought on foot.

Then came a warrior people on horseback, most likely the Blackfoot, and they drove the Shoshonis back south. They added their art to the display, of a style similar to that depicted on their hide paintings. The whole huge natural gallery shows the gradual march of time from prehistory through the coming of the horse and well into the advent of European trade and settlement. There is even a scene that shows a hanging, with a flag fluttering from a mast beside a gallows, and another of a figure or two in uniform that must represent Mounted Police.

The carvings and paintings, so dramatically illustrating warrior figures, animals, and scenes of the hunt and battle, number nearly sixty individual displays. Some of the oldest carvings may have weathered completely away.

Many of the scenes depicted on the sandstone are very extensive, and must have required several days to complete. The most detailed and the biggest one shows a battle with one hundred and fifteen warriors; seventy-one of them are attacking a camp of twenty-four tipis pitched in a circle. There are three ovals in the centre which apparently are earthworks sheltering a number of people. The attackers are accompanied by horses pulling travois. Warriors on the rim of the camp are firing with fourteen rifles at the attackers, and some of the attacking force are armed with rifles. Two figures are engaged in close combat in the camp, one swinging a tomahawk at a gun-bearing opponent.

So far, nobody has ever found evidence of a campsite here. Certainly there are no sites like the tipi villages along the Oldman River in the region of the Porcupine Hills, a three-days' ride to the northwest, which are marked by the circles of stones that held the lodges down in the wind. If there were camps here, they were those of small parties sleeping out for a short period of time on the prairie. Perhaps individuals searching for a dream to point their way came here alone to commune with the spirits of people gone before. After they had looked at the paintings and carvings for a while, perhaps they felt sufficiently inspired to add one of their own to the collection.

This unique natural gallery of the art of the Indian people is now preserved at Writing-on-Stone Provincial Park for as long as the elements will allow.

The great ocean of grass that reached across the Great Plains east of the Rockies invited cattle-ranchers farther and farther north to take advantage of the free range for their stock. The only law in the area was the six-shooters they packed on their belts and the rifles in their saddle scabbards. It was a wild frontier, where the Indians were treated not much better than the wolves which had turned to the cattle taking the place of the buffalo. In turn, as wolves became a menace, bounty-hunters named "wolfers" moved into the country, proving to be somewhat rough-and-ready visitors.

About the same time as the American cattlemen began showing up on the border area of the Canadian prairies (the first drive into Alberta coming from Washington via the Crow's Nest Pass in 1870), the Americans began enforcing the law to stop the trading of whiskey to the Indians. So the traders in Montana promptly headed north into Canada, where there were no police. Two traders, John J. Healy and Alfred B. Hamilton, built Fort Hamilton on the St. Mary's River a few miles upstream from its confluence with the Oldman. There they set up a trade with the Blood Indians, as well as with the scattering of thirty white settlers in the region. It was a crude fort, and the following year they proceeded to build a much stronger replacement near the same location out of hand-hewn cottonwood logs cut from the big trees along the river. It was a defensive stronghold, designed to easily hold the traders and their crew of about thirty men, and the mentality was defensive too. The Indians were allowed into the central square, but not into the store from which the trading was done. They passed their furs and buffalo robes in through a small opening and received their whiskey and goods in exchange. At no time were they allowed inside the store.

The trade goods came up from Fort Benton, Montana, which was supplied by sternwheel steamers slapping their way west from St. Louis along the Missouri river. At Fort Benton they were loaded into big freight wagons drawn by ox teams, three wagons to a hitch pulled by eight to ten big steers working in pairs with yokes on their necks. During the 1870s these bull teams hauled an average of three and a half million pounds of freight a year north to Fort Whoop-up and other posts scattered throughout the country, and came back with about twenty-five thousand buffalo robes annually.

The story goes that Fort Whoop-up got its name shortly after it was built when a string of ox teams were coming to the fort from the south. They were only a few miles out, it had been a very hot day, the oxen were tired and the drivers ready to camp, when somebody said if they whooped-'er-up and pushed the teams hard they could reach the fort that evening. One of the teamsters was a Frenchman, who was learning his English one word at a time. He took hold by yelling "Whoop-up" to his team and kept it up till they finally got to the fort. It was such a joke that somebody suggested the new post should be called Fort Whoop-up and the name stuck.

As far as iniquity, drunken brawls, and general uproar were concerned, Fort Whoop-up was no better or no worse than any other trading-post in the West at that time. Certainly, the Hudson's Bay Company forts to the north were all trading liquor to the Indians, but that did not deter them from sending some lurid and hair-raising stories of the doings of the American desperados they deemed intruders into Canada. No doubt Indians under the influence of cheap alcohol could be unpredictable and destructive; some were killed, but probably more often by other Indians than by whites, and rarely by the traders themselves. The traders, after all, were enterprising and acquisitive entrepreneurs who were fully aware that a dead Indian was a total loss as a customer.

There was a very prolific writer, a lady by the name of Agnes M. Laut, who was writing about the frontier of that time and her accounts were, if nothing else, not very accurate. She had a penchant for asking good questions of the wrong people – few of whom missed an opportunity to pass on fiction for profound fact. In any event, one way and another stories of wild orgies and drunken debauchery, well laced with gunsmoke and bloody murder, filtered through to the capital at Ottawa. And when, to the east of Fort Whoop-up, in the Cypress Hills, a gang of American wolfers massacred thirty-six Assiniboine people, public opinion back east was ready to be properly outraged.

In due course, a small force of two hundred men under Colonel James F. Macleod was dispatched west to establish law and order, its first duty being to capture the infamous Fort Whoop-up. Their journey from the head of the Great Lakes that spring and summer of 1874 was long and arduous, over country that none of them had ever seen before. These men of the grandly named North West Mounted Police were young, adventurous types, none of them less than five foot ten inches tall and no strangers to horses. Dressed in heavy wool uniforms, they suffered acutely from the sun and the chafing of their saddles. By the time they reached Fort Garry, south of Lake Winnipeg, they were fully and very uncomfortably acquainted with mosquitoes and blackflies. And doubtless they were somewhat appalled at the immensity of the country before them – some eight hundred miles of it to Fort Whoop-up.

Colonel Macleod must have been troubled, for he did not know anything of the strength of that garrison, or, if it came to a fight, how his green troops would conduct themselves under fire. Somewhere out in what is now Saskatchewan, Macleod got horribly lost.

How the force could lose direction so thoroughly is something of a
mystery, for they must have had maps, however crude, as well as a
compass, and there was the sun and stars to go by. But get lost they
did, in a big way, for they eventually found themselves at Fort
Benton on the Missouri River. The Colonel's luck was not all bad,
for there he found Jerry Potts, a half-breed with a very good reputation as a warrior and scout, and promptly hired him as guide for the
Force.

Potts, of Blood Indian and Scots parentage, was famous among
the Blackfoot Nation as a great warrior. He was also a man of few
words, with a genius for reducing and interpreting a long-winded
speech to a single sentence. At one time during his service with the
Mounted Police, Colonel Macleod met with a Blackfoot chief who
proceeded to make a long, emphatic speech that lasted about half an
hour. At its conclusion, the Colonel turned to Potts and asked what
he had said. Potts told him, "He t'inks you are one hell of a man!"
As they rode northwest toward Fort Whoop-up in that summer of
1874, the Colonel was getting a bit anxious about how close they
were; when they came to a hill, he asked his guide what they would
see when they got to the top. Potts grunted and said, "Nudder
hill!"

When they finally did ride out onto the rim of the St. Mary's
Valley above the strongly built fort, the Colonel proceeded to
deploy his men in as good a position as possible, with their single
cannon loaded and pointed in the right direction. Then he and Potts
rode over to the gate and knocked loudly. For a while there wasn't a
sound. Then the gate was opened a crack and a scared-looking half-
breed guard scuttled out and away into the brush by the river. The
fort was empty. Leaving a notice posted on the gate, the Colonel
camped close by on the flat.

In due course, he met Hamilton and his partner, John Healy, as
well as several others of the crew. When Macleod offered to buy the
fort, Hamilton asked for more than he felt obliged to pay. So he

took his men on west to camp on an island on the Oldman, where he proceeded to build a stout fort, which he called Fort Macleod.

The liquor trade was stopped. The traders hung on for a while, but the buffalo were pretty much gone, and this business also came to an end. It was thus that law and order came to the western Canadian prairies largely ahead of settlement, for, apart from a few cattlemen and traders, there was still nobody but Indians in the whole region.

Right from the start, the North West Mounted Police played no favourites, being impartial to both white men and Indians. When a recently arrived American rancher left a pair of pants on the seat of one of his wagons and came back later to find his garment stolen, he rode down to the fort to report the theft. When he asked permission to shoot the thief, the commanding officer in charge fixed him with cold blue eyes and told him that if he shot an Indian, or anyone else, he would be arrested, tried for murder, and, if found guilty, hung by the neck until dead.

Conversely, when a Blood brave killed a cow belonging to a rancher, two constables rode out to a big camp of Bloods on the Waterton River, and then boldly went right in among a swarm of angry armed warriors and arrested him. It was a moment fraught with possible bloodshed, but the sheer guts of the policemen so impressed the Indians that nothing happened. There was nothing the Blackfoot admired more than courage, and these uniformed warriors of the Queen were not short of it.

Following Custer's defeat at the Battle of the Little Bighorn, Sitting Bull fled to Canada with his Sioux people and camped just east of Cypress Hills. They stayed there for a considerable time, until finally an agreement was made between the two governments to move them back to the United States. Under escort of an N.W.M.P. corporal and a constable, the Sioux, numbering several hundred people, moved back south across the border to a spot on the Milk River just inside Montana and east of the Sweetgrass Hills.

There they camped to wait for the American cavalry unit that was to take charge, but when they failed to show up, the constable was dispatched to find them. After considerable riding, he came up to a fair-sized detachment of the Seventh Cavalry Regiment. The officer commanding it inquired where the Canadian force was located, and who was the commanding officer. He was somewhat amazed when the constable told him that the corporal was back in camp with the Sioux, and that was all the force there was.

It was thus that the North West Mounted Police won the reputation that became famous throughout the world, and that has followed through to modern times under the name of the Royal Canadian Mounted Police. With only a relative handful of men patrolling an enormous area reaching from the 49th parallel to the Arctic, they won and held a respect that has served this country well.

Colonel Macleod's command in those first years on the prairies was helped immeasurably by the services of Jerry Potts, the tough, courageous scout who knew the Indians through and through. More than once he saved patrols from probable death in cold winter blizzards, guided them on the invisible trails of erring thieves, and generally won the deep respect of the Colonel and his men. At times, he was also the cause of some humour.

On one occasion he had taken his wife and family by wagon down to Fort Benton to buy some supplies. At the trading-store his wife purchased a very ornately decorated child's chamber-potty made of china that took her eye. She had no idea what it was, no doubt considering it a white man's version of a big teacup, to be used on very special occasions, but she prized it highly and wrapped it well to protect it from being broken on the return journey to their cabin on the Belly River. There she placed it in a prominent place on a shelf, where she could admire it as she did her housework.

Some time later, Colonel Macleod had occasion to ride into that part of the Blood reserve to meet with one of the chiefs, and he went first to pick up his interpreter. It was a hot summer day when he rode up to Jerry Potts's cabin and he asked for a drink of water. Mrs. Potts duly fetched him a drink, fresh from the spring not far away, and held it up to him very proudly in the china potty as he sat on his horse with the rest of his patrol at his back. The Colonel's momentary surprise was well hidden; without batting an eye, he had a good drink and passed the "cup" back with a smile and his thanks. The sergeant beside him sat stiffly on his horse at rigid attention, looking straight ahead, his choked-up mirth only given away by a slight flicker of his features at the corners of his mouth. Needless to say, when the story got back to barracks, it caused a roar of laughter that echoed through the whole fort.

Thanks to Macleod and his men, the early settlers along the Old-man and its tributaries did not have to wear the law in a holster. When an American cowboy came north with a trail herd and rode into a Canadian town with a six-shooter hanging on his belt, all set for a noisy celebration, he was promptly relieved of its weight; and if he ever saw it again, he was very lucky indeed.

The old wild, free days of the Blackfoot were clearly gone, and in 1877 a treaty was signed with the leading chiefs, and the tribes were given reservations. But when the Métis cut loose during the Riel Rebellion to take over lands they figured belonged to them, it was very dangerous; for if the Indians had joined the rebels, settlement would have been set back for years. But all of the Indians, including the Blackfoot, remained loyal, thanks to a few influential and respected missionaries, plus the firmness and fairness of the N.W.M.P.

A new kind of civilization had come to the Canadian territories to stay. The Indians were confined to reservations and the white cattle-ranchers were the new kings of the prairies.

8 *Cowboy Days*

The cattlemen drawn by this bountiful expanse of grass drove herds into the Oldman River country from the south. The herds were miles long, plodding ten to fifteen miles a day, and they were driven by crews of cowboys with their attendant chuckwagons carrying food and blanket-rolls through grass that waved stirrup-deep in the wind. These were a tough, hard-working, colourful breed of men – survivor types ready for anything the country and the climate could throw at them.

Like all mounted men, they had that certain arrogance of bearing that went with their range-bred horses, and the horses were every bit as tough and independent as their riders. The big, open sky was their roof, the grass their feed, and they knew no confinement of fences except the portable corrals made of a single strand of rawhide supported by guyed stakes that were used to hold them when a change of mounts was required. There wasn't a barbed-wire fence from the North Pole for as far as a man could ride through the prairies, hills, and mountains deep into Mexico.

At first the cowboys were mostly American, coming from every state in the Union, and they included every kind of character, from outlaws to aristocrats, ragamuffins wearing tattered garments to dandies in buckskins and broadcloth with silver gleaming on their riding-gear. There were those who couldn't write their own names, and many who carried well-worn volumes of the literary classics in their war-bags, which they read over and over when opportunity afforded. They all had two things in common: they could ride, and they understood cattle. Some got by with horses more or less easy to sit, while others could do a day's work on top of equine man-eaters that knew every mean trick in the book. It was said of some that they could ride anything that wore hair, and it was not as much of an exaggeration as it sounds.

From the beginning, they were written about and talked about. Stories of their prowess with ropes and guns were told around campfires in the wilderness and across the world in cottage and castle alike. Part of their world were the folk-songs of derring-do, pathos, and romance that they sang to the cattle as they rode around sleeping herds on the bed grounds at night. Whether a man was as skilled as an opera singer or had a voice like a frog, this singing to the cattle was an important, soothing link of communication between man and beast, helping to prevent the dreaded stampedes that always cost heavily in pounds of beef, and were sometimes fatal to cowboys. They were a reckless, hard-working, hard-playing lot, these men, and I got acquainted as a young man with enough of the old-timers to know that they deserved their legends.

When the rolling hills and prairies of the Oldman River basin were first used as range by these American ranchers, the market for beef in Canada was limited by what little the Indian Department bought under a skimpy budget to feed the hungry Indians and by the tiny amount of meat used in local consumption. But in 1884 the Canadian Pacific Railway reached Calgary and the Rockies to open up the market, and the Canadian beef industry began to bloom.

Investors from the eastern provinces and Britain were attracted by the lure of this seemingly limitless expanse of grass that ripened on the stem and could sustain cattle all winter. Here and there in sheltered pockets among the foothills and along the valleys the log buildings of permanent homesteads – the headquarters of the various ranches – began to show up, each one with cattle and horse brands registered in the territorial office. Eighteen eighty-three was the year that my grandfather began building his ranch in the Oldman basin, where Pothole Creek ran into the St. Mary's River, and began to raise cattle.

The livestock ran free on the range, being held more or less within the unfenced boundaries of the ranches by the cowboys, but inevitably there was a certain intermingling of herds. So twice a year the cattle were gathered in organized round-ups under the direction of a chosen captain, with riders from every ranch in the locality representing the brands they rode for. Each rider needed from eight to ten saddle-horses, for the work went on from daylight to dark, with a possible break in the middle of the day during hot weather. The spring round-up was for branding calves born that year, while the fall round-up was directed toward gathering beef bound for market, generally four-year-old steers and dry cows. Depending on its size, each round-up crew was accompanied by one or more chuckwagons, each driven by a cook.

The cattle were dependent on range grass the year around, though following the fall weaning most ranches bunched their young stock close to headquarters, where they could be fed during hard winter weather. Because cattle did not have the buffalo's natural habit of facing the wind and brushing down through the snow with their heads for feed, heavy losses occurred during severe blizzards about every ten years. The thin-skinned, long-horned cattle from the south were particularly vulnerable. They would drift with the wind, sometimes into a cul-de-sac in a deep draw where they would freeze solid standing up in temperatures that dropped to forty or fifty below and wind-chill that could be much lower.

One blizzard that struck in early October caught a herd recently arrived from the south. In spite of hard riding by the crew looking after them, they turned their tails to the north wind, pointed their noses in the direction of balmy Texas and drifted. All the cowboys finally gave up and sought shelter but one – John Ware, a Negro who was a great rider and an easy-going man well liked by all. When the storm let up on the third day, all the cows were long gone and there was still no sign of the missing cowboy or his horse. They looked for him, but finally gave him up for lost.

The two owners of the cattle rode south looking for the missing herd. Two days out, they ran into a stage-driver, who reported that a herd had been seen, accompanied by a rider. This made them wonder if somebody had taken advantage of the storm to rustle their cattle and hide them away in some hidden pocket in the hills. The drifting snow left no sign of a trail. On the evening of the next day, it was snowing again as they rode out on the rim overlooking the Oldman River valley. There were fresh cow-tracks in the snow, and they could see a fire on the edge of a grove of cottonwoods. As they approached with guns loose in their holsters, they saw a man turn from the fire to face them. For a tense moment they watched him, and then they recognized the missing John Ware. He was busy roasting a haunch of venison from a deer he had killed, and the feeling of gladness was mutual all around. As they got stiffly down from their horses to join him at the fire, they looked about them, and as far as they could see up and down the valley, cattle were grazing. They shared John's supper, while he told of drifting with the cattle for two days and two nights of riding and working to keep them together. His face was wind-burnt and frost-bitten, but his grin was as wide and cheery as ever. The whole herd was safe here where the snow was not as deep and they were out of the wind. Right there John Ware got a raise in his wages.

Later John Ware settled down to ranch in the Oldman country, near Turner Valley and then at a ranch near Brooks. According to legend, he is credited with being the first settler to notice the presence of oil through seepage in the area – oil that in 1914 produced the oil boom in Turner Valley and Black Diamond, with wild shanty-towns springing up with names like "Little Chicago".

They were an impressively tough, enterprising lot, these cattle-men who took over the great grasslands from the Indians. In the country up along the Oldman above the three forks just east of the mountains, some of the ranchers were British army officers retired from service in India, members of wealthy families in England and steeped in the traditions of aristocracy. They built big, well-furnished homes of logs and stone, solid and comfortable. Later, it was in this area that the Prince of Wales established his ranch near the Highwood River.

There were others of British extraction, some of whom owned land temporarily, who generally were not known for their prac-ticality. These were "remittance men", black sheep of wealthy families, who had been sent to the colonies with a quarterly stipend to sustain them – and to keep them as far away as possible. Some steadied down to become respected citizens, and others squandered their money in colourful ways, finally fading into obscurity. But they all made an important contribution to a part of the country where money was scarce, for they generally spent theirs like water.

All these ranchers had something in common with the Indians, for their lives were totally dependent on horses, which they rode or drove in harness. Most of them would not walk from the house to the barn if there was a horse to ride, and usually there was one handy. Youngsters born on the ranches generally rode before they could walk. Because it was not considered genteel for them to ride astride, the ladies of some of the families in the higher strata of society rode side-saddle. The more practical ones adopted regular stock saddles, wore heavy, long divided skirts, and rode astride like men. For the most part, they were excellent riders, and some of them could handle cattle and even use a rope or a gun.

One lady who came north with her husband and a herd of cattle to take up a ranch had spent her younger years riding with him in a touring wild-west show. She was a very independent, no-nonsense type who could handle herself in just about every kind of circum-stance. Once, when her husband was away on business, she caught a neighbour helping himself to firewood out of a dead stand of trees in the valley below the ranch buildings. She waited till he got his wagon all loaded, then rode up and accosted him. He was very cheeky about it, grinning as he started his team toward home. But the grin rapidly faded when she reached into a saddle-bag, drew a six-shooter, cocked it with an ominous click, and pointed it un-waveringly at his belt buckle. Then she ordered him to drive to the ranch buildings, where she made him unload the wood and stack it neatly. It was a chastened, very respectful man who finally slunk off in the direction of his home.

The heartland of the old ranching frontier from the earliest days down to the present was the foothill country around the Oldman. Life for the early pioneer cattlemen was hard, but it had its frivolous moments.

On one occasion, Sam Howe, a colourful, hard-riding rancher, brought his crew into town after a long, hot, and dusty round-up to give them a chance to unwind. This they proceeded to do with great enthusiasm at the local hotel, until in the course of the festivities one cowboy passed out so completely that everyone present became concerned. He was duly examined, pronounced dead, and then laid out in state in a makeshift coffin. A wake was then held which went on till sunrise.

A funeral for their deceased comrade was organized, a flatbed rack on a wagon was brought to serve as a hearse, and a grave was dug in the cemetery. Then the funeral procession, complete with a long column of pall-bearers and mourners, headed for the graveyard. When they reached the graveside, it was very hot, and everyone was thirsty, so all and sundry left to go back to the hotel for refresh-ments, leaving the hearse standing unattended by the open grave. After a while, "the body" stirred in the casket and then sat up, rubbed its eyes, and looked around. Even in the throes of a horren-dous hangover, it was easy for the cowboy to take in the details of his surroundings – the freshly dug grave and the headstones of preceding unfortunates and the general aspects of a funeral which,

from the way he felt, was obviously supposed to be his. He shud-
dered, climbed shakily out of the coffin and down to the ground,
and went for his horse. He left riding west for British Columbia on
the other side of the mountains. It was said that he was a total
abstainer for the rest of his life.

The Indians have always been noted for their inability to handle
liquor, but some later white-skinned arrivals were no more immune
to alcohol. Some of them made a habit of stealing other people's
horses and cattle, too, with no compunction about the rules of the
game. All of which kept the Mounted Police busy, and resulted in
the building of some very escape-proof jails wherein to keep those
unlucky enough to get caught.

When Louis Riel's band of Métis revolted and, with the help of
some Crees, proceeded to kill some people at Frog Lake, and a number of Mounted Police in another skirmish, the whole plains country of western Canada was in an uproar. Various groups of volunteer
rangers were organized in the ranching country to patrol and guard
the scattered communities of settlers, for it was feared that the
Blackfoot warriors would join the Métis and Crees in a general up-
rising. But, thanks to the influence of the chiefs and the general
respect for the Mounted Police – along with the valuable help of two
missionaries, the Reverend McDougall and Father Lacombe – the
Indians around the Oldman remained at peace. It was, nevertheless,
a very anxious time, for the scattered population of white settlers
was extremely vulnerable if the Indians had chosen to go on the
warpath.

However, there was justified bitterness among the Indians. A few
years earlier they had been free-roaming hunter-gatherers living off
the buffalo, and now they were confined to reservations as wards of
the government, dependent on inadequate hand-outs of beef from
government agents who were sometimes downright dishonest.
When a hungry Peigan killed a rancher's cow and was arrested, he
gave testimony at his trial that the white man had killed the
Indians' buffalo without permission, and asked why he was not allowed to kill a cow. Presenting the hide with its brand, the police

explained he could not kill the cow because it was branded with the mark of the owner. The prisoner reflected on this and said, "We should have branded the buffalo."

The Indian did not always understand the law, though it is amazing how much he respected it. He did not comprehend, for instance, that a man arrested by the police was innocent until proved guilty by trial in court. In the old days under the laws of the tribes, he had revered and lived by the decrees of the chiefs and band councils. Now he saw governing white men breaking their own laws, and there were too many times when they got away with it, in a totally confusing hodge-podge of manipulation. To him the white man's law was something of an enigma, though it could be fatally efficient.

There was Charcoal, a Peigan warrior, who caught his wife making love with a fellow tribesman. In a fit of understandable rage, he blew his wife's lover off her body with a shot through the head. Had he gone and given himself up to the police, he likely would have gone free, after the discomfort of staying in jail waiting for trial. At that time there were no Indian lawyers to represent him or to give him advice, and he did not speak or understand English. He was sick with tuberculosis, and he believed that the only honourable thing left for him to do was to go on the war trail toward inevitable death, and take as many high-ranking white men with him as possible to the spirit world.

First, he ambushed the reservation agent at his home, but the bullet meant to kill him only broke his arm. Accompanied by his wife and her sister, Charcoal proceeded to run away up onto the heavily timbered heights of the Porcupine Hills overlooking the Oldman River valley. His camp there was eventually located by a group of police officers and their Indian scouts in the late evening of a cold, snowy fall day. But before they could close in, he got the women away to the horses and escaped in a blaze of rifle fire.

Under cover of the storm, he made his way south. The continuing pursuit under bad conditions was not very well organized. Though the Peigans were not altogether sympathetic to him, they did not totally co-operate with the police, either. Back and forth between the Oldman and the border the chase continued, following rumour as much as fact. There was another shoot-out in a camp on the upper reaches of the Belly River in thick timber, from which Charcoal got clean away with his two women. Half starved, cold, sick, and totally desperate, he continued to elude his pursuers for weeks.

At one point in the hunt, he rode right into the police head-quarters at Fort Macleod looking for a chance to kill the command-ing officer. But he settled for stealing a highly prized, very fast horse and made a run back up the Oldman, eluding the astonished police officers who were trying to cut him off. Meanwhile, his women had abandoned him, and he was all alone.

At a spot south of the Oldman near the Waterton River, Sergeant Wilde of the N.W.M.P. saw him and rode hard to intercept him. Bravely, but very foolishly, the officer rode right up to him, where-upon Charcoal shot him out of his saddle and escaped again. Finally, exhausted and starving, he rode back to his home cabin on the reserve, where he was overwhelmed by his own people, tied up, and turned over to the police. He was subsequently tried for mur-der, pronounced guilty, and hanged. But he hasn't been forgotten, for his defiant feat of endurance was magnificent in spite of its utter tragic futility. When he was captured, the ranching country up along the Oldman generally breathed a sigh of relief and everyone in the outlying areas slept much better at night.

The railways had brought not only a market for the ranchers' beef, but also people who would compete for the ranchers' land. Homesteaders were trickling into the country, filing claims on open land. The old days of wide-open range were going, as barbed-wire fences were being built to mark the boundaries of deeded land and some of the grazing leases. In an attempt to keep these "sodbusters" out, many of the ranchers made contracts with their working cow-boys and trusted friends to file on quarter sections of 160 acres within their holdings, prove them up by occupancy and whatever cultivation was necessary by law, and then sell them back to the rancher at a pre-arranged price. It was illegal, but the officials tended to be more sympathetic to the old ranchers than to the new-comers, and generally looked the other way. Some enterprising characters took up homesteads with no other intention than to cash in on their nuisance value.

One such man filed on a homestead with a good spring right in the middle of the Waldron Ranching Company's range. Suspecting him of cattle-rustling and general thievery, but unable to catch him in the act, the ranch manager reported him to the police. Mean-while, this intruder had been working for the police, building a new barracks at Fort Macleod. His acquisitive eye noticed a new stove sitting in its crate, where it had been unloaded on an open lot not far from headquarters. Every time he passed it, he poured some water on it, and slowly removed the crate piece by piece until the stove sat alone and abandoned among the weeds and grass, looking like a rusted-out hulk.

One day he walked into headquarters to ask the commanding officer what he wanted for that old stove out on the back lot. That worthy knew nothing of an old stove, so he went out to look, and, being too busy to examine it closely, he told the conniver he could have it for nothing if he would take it away. It duly arrived in the homesteader's cabin, where, after some diligent cleaning and polishing, it stood in shining splendour.

Some time later this same officer had occasion to call at this man's place, looking for information about stolen cattle. He was cordially invited into the cabin for coffee, where he noticed the new stove. Something about it bothered the policeman, for they were missing a new kitchen range at headquarters, and he asked where it had come from. His host told him, "Oh, that's the old stove you gave me. I scrubbed it and polished it up and it looks great – just like new!" The officer left with the distinct impression that he had been had.

The Waldron Ranch finally bought this rascal out at its price, under the thinly veiled threat of hanging him to the nearest tree if he did not accept.

Life in the ranching country was anything but dull, despite the amenities of life that were missing on account of remoteness, and the limitations that markets put upon the residents. In due course, a church was built – one of the first in the territory, which was located under a ridge between the middle and north forks of the Oldman east of the Livingstone Range, and more or less in the middle of the far-flung community. Small one-room schools were also constructed here and there, within riding distance of various ranches. These were generally presided over by young ladies who were high-school graduates with a permit to teach. Like the students they taught, they rode back and forth to school from the homes where they boarded. There was a considerable turnover among these ladies, for single women were scarce, and the cowboys and young home-steaders wanted wives to brighten their lives and help them carve out a living.

Despite the turnover in teachers, these schools provided the children with the opportunity to learn the basics of reading, writing, and mathematics, with a smattering of history and geography thrown in. Successful pursuit of the basics of the three R's – reading, writing and 'rithmetic – was really all they needed to pursue any further education they wished.

No matter where their homes might be along the river or up on one of its lesser tributaries, the white settlers were just as deeply in-fluenced by the spirit of the free-flowing water as the Indians who preceded them. In winter, the Oldman was frozen in shackles of ice, silent and gleaming in its coating of armour on which people skated and held picnics on warmer days. Sometimes in spring the ice went out with a grinding roar that was awesome in its power. And occa-sionally, in flood time, riders attempting to swim their mounts across it got into trouble and drowned. In summer, it murmured serenely as it flowed down between its banks. Youngsters and their parents fished and swam in it, perhaps taking it for granted, but loving it just the same.

Sometimes one of the ranch families would pack up some camp-ing gear and food and ride up through the Gap on a holiday trip among the mountains. When they saw the big pile of prayer rocks left by uncounted generations of Indians before them, no doubt some of them knew the significance of this stone pile and told it to their children around the evening campfire. So the legend of the stones did not die, though nobody placed much historical value on them, nor did anybody feel deeply enough about it to add another rock to the pile. It would have been contrary to the concept of Christian ethics to pay homage to a small-g Peigan god. They did not realize that the Indians and Christian white people were really worshipping the same God. The only difference was that the Indians believed that their Old Man was manifest in all nature – in the rocks, plants, animals, and every detail of the world they knew. They did not have the written words of prophets and scholars that Christians follow; the writing that they knew and revered had been done by nature. Their noses picked up the smell of the river – the blending of sage, willows, cottonwoods, flowers, and earth rich with the coolness of rain – their ears the sound of the wind and the water, and their skins the warmth of the sun. They had named the river the Oldman because they thought he must live there, it was so beautiful.

While the white people saw the river's beauty, too, they did not recognize the depth of its signficance. Few of them realized that if it was to last, it must be guarded and preserved as the key to the bounty of the land on which they lived.

And so they went on tending their horses and cattle, making a living, suffering keenly on occasion, but also sometimes seeing their dreams fulfilled. They were a scattered few in a vast stretch of hills, prairies, and mountains, where deep-rooted trees sang with the wind and the grass waved in accompaniment. They worked hard, and they played hard on occasion; and strangely enough it was in the play that this community achieved a measure of recognition throughout the world.

As I have said, some of these ranchers were retired British army officers who had served in India. There they had enjoyed playing

polo, the game of all games in that country, and they soon introduced it to the country of the Oldman. Under the excellent coach-
ing of the old army players, teams were organized, which met on
various suitably prepared playing-grounds on the ranches. The sons
of these pioneers and the working cowboys took to this game with
enthusiasm, and so did their cow-horses. These tough native cayuse-
bred mounts, some of them with a measure of thoroughbred blood
in their veins, could run for hours, turn on a silver dollar, and chase
a ball at top speed from a one-jump start. Compared to the sleek,
pampered mounts ridden in polo in more sophisticated surroundings, these range-bred horses were a rough-looking lot – some of
them looked like the wrath of God. But their legs were strong, they
were as quick as cats on their feet, and their hearts had boundless
endurance. Some of the polo-playing cowboys rode their favourite
mounts twenty miles to a game, played it at top speed, and then
rode back home on the same horse.

The North Fork Polo Team based in High River played against
all comers and by the late years of the last century were the best in
Canada. They were looking for heavier competition, so when they
received an invitation to go to California and play in an international polo meet there, they loaded their horses and equipment
on railway cars and headed south.

When they arrived, their mounts and well-used equipment were
something of a contrast to the high-bred polo ponies and tack of the
competition, and the newcomers from Canada were the butts of
considerable good-natured joking among the high-society Americans. But when the games began, the atmosphere changed rapidly,
for the Canadians were hard-riding devils on horseback and their
hard-bitten ponies ran circles around the opposition. The Canadian
team took the cup and in 1905 won the North American champion-
ship. In due course they went abroad to meet the best teams of England, Argentina, Egypt, and India. Wherever they played, people
used to the elegant world of polo were amazed at this odd-looking
outfit. But once the playing started, it was the same story over
again: they rode the competition into the ground, and won the

hearts of spectators and opposing players alike for their enthusiasm and good-sportsmanship. They came back home triumphant with the World Cup – a feat that no polo team in Canada has ever come close to duplicating.

But during the early years of the century, ranching country was changing. The dryland country was filling up with homesteaders encouraged by federal policies, and the newcomers put a strain on the water resources, and altered the pattern of grazing leases. Soon the cattle-ranching business resolved into properties, most of which were fenced. No longer did the big round-up crews go on the biannual gatherings. The whole beef-raising business was changing –and it was dealt a terrible blow by the winter of 1906–7 when the chinook never came to provide relief, and the cattle died in their thousands.

When the First World War broke out in 1914, most of the able-bodied young men of the West, mindful of their links with Britain, answered the call to arms by joining various artillery and cavalry units. Along with thousands of range-bred horses, they shipped out to fight in the bloody battlefields of France. There the old rules of war did not apply, but it took the generals some time to realize it. Pitting men on horses against artillery and machine-guns resulted in carnage such as the world had never seen; it was pure hell for the men and even worse for their mounts and the artillery teams that pulled the big guns into position. Many letters home had sad words for the ill-fed horses that were slaughtered in battle, to be replaced by other horses, most of them bewildered by the change from the still air of the foothills to the muddy bedlam of Flanders.

Two thousand volunteers from the Oldman country marched out of Lethbridge with the 20th Battery. Only four of the original draft came back unscathed. The rest were either killed or put out of action by wounds. Among the men were some warriors of the Blackfoot people, who gave excellent account of themselves.

The rangeland and farming country's character was never quite the same again, but the Oldman flowed on; for those few who returned, a link with a happier time.

9 *The Living River*

Roderick Haig-Brown has said, "A river never sleeps," and he wrote a big book with that title which is not only a literary classic but profoundly true. He was a great fly fisherman, and the author of several fine books on fishing, but one does not have to be a devotee of this sport to love a river. Nor does one have to be a philosopher to appreciate the tremendous range of a river's influence. The Indians saw and understood the Oldman's influence on their lives so deeply that the prayer stones they had left, one by one, till they were heaped up in that great pile beside the river represented the prayers of uncounted generations of their people.

But a mere fifty-odd years ago, during the height of the Great Depression, we came along and built a big camp to house and feed three hundred or so unemployed men. We proceeded to turn the old Indian trail through the Gap into a narrow, twisting road to accommodate wheels. The road was built with picks, shovels, wheelbarrows, and sweat to the tune of a dollar a day per man, plus enough to eat. For men who knew real hunger and despair, it was welcome work. When they came to that pile of loose rocks nobody told them it was a historic monument. What they needed was rocks to make a roadbed to shovel into their wheelbarrows, and nobody could blame them for loading up and scattering uncounted thousands of those prayer rocks along the roadbed. It was an omen of what was to come in our treatment of the holy river of the Blackfoot people.

Thunder Mountain and the abrupt, towering cliffs facing it across the river are not changed. The pure limestone rock slides and great abutments are the same. But now there is the road, blasted and graded into the proportions of a highway, leading up the valley. Somewhere in its foundation are the prayer stones, no longer visible as a reminder of the spirit of the river. But they are still there, deep down, which is a bit of comfort to those of us travelling road 517 who know the story of this historic spot.

Nor has the river changed here where it flows and swirls around huge boulders through whitewater rapids and deep blue-green pools as clear as crystal in summer. During spring run-offs, floods rip and tear down this twisted channel, roaring with immense power that can be heard for miles on a still day. The water then is yellow-brown with mud and silt and carries along uprooted trees, brush, and driftwood. Its power varies from year to year according to the depth of the winter snow-pack upstream and the climate of the moment. Let three days of warm rain fall on a deep accumulation of winter snow and the result is awesome.

It is perhaps in fall, a gentle resting-time in prelude to the harshness of winter cold, when the aspens, willows, and cottonwoods are dressed in red and gold mixed with the deep green of the conifers, that the river is most spectacularly beautiful. Then peace seems to be carried on the spicy autumn air, a warm, confiding promise of another spring and summer to come. The character of a truly wild, free-flowing river has a multitude of shining facets that reflect not only the power of the sun but the hosts of life in and along it.

I was born in 1915 near the ranch my grandfather established in the rolling hills at the confluence of Pothole Creek and the St. Mary's as they flow towards the Oldman near Lethbridge. When I was four,

my family moved west to a ranch my father had bought in the foothills near the forks of Drywood Creek, a tributary of the Waterton
River. It was a wonderful place – and a wonderful time – to be a boy
running free. The mountains here were only two miles away, and
the cold, clear water came leaping down Drywood Creek in playful
abandon, inviting me and my brother John to play, and fish, and be
alone, and fall in love with mountain rivers.

Those of us lucky enough to grow up along the Oldman and its
tributaries there in the shadow of the Rockies were truly blessed,
though many of us did not realize it then. We knew that these
rivers could be dangerous. A few of us met the end of our trail when
we slipped from some insecure perch above its flood, or rode into it
on a horse that proved unable to swim. Horses that grow up following their mothers as sucking colts by a river can generally swim like
beavers; but some of those raised in the highlands never learn to
swim. For a rider to find this out in swift, ice-cold water is
sometimes much too late.

By the same token, some of us learned to swim and some of us
failed. But that did not deter us from fishing and exploring. We
loved to wander the streams in pursuit of trout. For a rod, we generally made do with a slim peeled-willow pole with a line tied to its
tip and a hook baited with anything from a bloody fragment of unlucky gopher to a grasshopper. It did not matter to the unsophis-
ticated, hungry trout; all we had to do was stalk and locate the prey
in some hold in the lee of a rock or under an overhanging bank and
present the bait without showing our moving shadows.

Caught fish were strung on a forked willow stick and duly presented to our mothers, who were generally delighted. There is nothing in the way of fish that can equal fresh-caught mountain trout
cleaned, rolled in flour or cornmeal, and fried in butter to make a
delicious meal. And we youngsters knew the deep, primitive satisfaction of hunter-gatherers contributing food for our families.

Sometimes we caught more than fish in the river. One summer
evening when I was riding along the Drywood to bring in the milk

cows, I came on a somewhat portly gentleman in long waders sitting in the middle of the fast stream. The waders were awash and it was clear that he was pinned down by the weight of the water, in grave danger of being swept into a deeper pool, where he would sink like a stone.

I was just a kid, and had no hope of dragging him out to safety. But my wiry cow-pony and my rope had exciting possibilities. I splashed my horse toward him and sent a loop sailing out over his head, and jerked it shut around him. Dallying my rope around the saddle-horn, I headed my horse for the bank, with the bedraggled fisherman bouncing along behind, much to his surprise. He was even more surprised when he came to a halt on the bank with his head below his feet, a circumstance that left him inundated by the gallons of water issuing from his waders. When he came to his feet, he was not obviously aware of my good intentions; my horse took one look at him and bolted.

That was how I met the Judge, a salty-tongued Scotsman and a true fishing enthusiast, with really good fly-fishing tackle that somehow escaped the roping adventure. It was not to survive a visit a few days later from Butcher, a neighbouring rancher. Butcher arrived in his new car, which he drove grandly up to visit the Judge's tent beside the river – and which, after a convivial visit with lots of whiskey imbibed, he reversed grandly, insisting all the time that he was in low gear, right across the Judge's tent and fine split-cane rod. Since I was sitting in the car at the time, as a youthful passenger, the incident made a strong impression on me, especially as we proceeded to reverse right down the six-foot bank and fall with a crash into the river. Butcher made to get out, but the water lapping over the floorboards dissuaded him, and he drove along the riverbed until he could swing out at a low point in the bank. It was an interesting incident, and gave me further memories of the river and the people to be met along it.

We all had our work to do helping on the various ranches where we lived, but we used the spare time well. Some of us were more

venturesome than others and were fond of going out on short camp-
ing-trips, pretending we were old frontiersmen living off the land.
We generally carried a small cotton sack with a bit of salt, a few
slices of bacon, perhaps a chunk of bread, and a few other odds and
ends. Matches were an important item, which we usually prepared
by dipping them in melted paraffin and then tying them in a
bundle with a piece of string. Such matches would light when
struck on a dry rock even in rain. A few of us mastered making a fire
with a fire-bow and drill, which can be made with the help of a
piece of stout cord just about anywhere there are trees. But it is a
slow way to make a fire – hard work for a youngster impatient with
hunger. Besides much muscle power, the right tinder is essential.
We knew why the old Indians carefully carried fire from camp to
camp in a hollow horn.

When we built our cooking-fire in the evening, we made it on a
suitable bedground, letting it burn down to a bed of coals just right
for grilling fish or perhaps a grouse. Sometimes we snared the
grouse, Indian-style, out of a tree with a noose of brass wire fastened
to the end of the fishing-pole. Some of us carried catapults made
with two rubber bands and a forked stick, with a leather pouch for a
stone. With some practice a hungry boy can knock a grouse on the
head at twenty feet with such a weapon. We either cooked our game
on a thin, flat rock over the fire, or we made a grid woven with
green willow; this not only served as a cooking utensil but also
smoked the food lightly as it cooked, making it delicious.

Sometimes, when we had the time, we used a different method
to deal with a big fish or a fairly heavy bird like a duck or a blue
grouse. We mixed some clay and water to a proper degree of sticki-
ness and carefully encased the bird or fish in it. Then we just buried
the mud cylinder in hot coals and gave it the time needed to cook.
To keep the thing from exploding, we stuck a hollow straw at each
end leading from the meat out. When the meat was ready, we
rolled the whole thing out of the fire and cracked the baked mud
away, which took the feathers and skin with it. Fish was excellent

cooked that way. As for duck, if the mud was worked well into the feathers there was no taste of them, and the meat was juicy and delicious. The shrivelled-up guts stayed inside the rib cage and were thrown away with the bones. In any case, the difference between good food and bad food is real hunger, and we boys were generally as hungry as wolves after a blizzard.

When supper was over, we rebuilt the fire for a while and let it burn down again. Then, using a flat rock or a suitable piece of wood, we scraped the coals and ashes to one side, leaving a patch of warm earth. We covered this with green boughs for a mattress and rolled up in our blankets on top of it – if we had any. So long as it stayed dry, we slept well, but if it rained, it was not very comfortable. If we didn't find enough to eat, it was worse. Then we came home soaked and starved, but we always had a story to tell. Somehow the discomfort of a wet camp was always forgotten when the sun came out again and the river beckoned once more.

A couple of us were far back in the mountains once when we lost our horses and failed to find anything to eat. We got around starvation and the utter exhaustion that was just as dangerous by eating ants, big juicy ants that tasted like gooseberries, which we dug out of rotten stumps. As I recall we ate some of their sweet-tasting white grubs as well. As any bear will testify, ants are a delicacy. Years later, it came to our attention that Indians sometimes stirred up a big ant-nest and trapped the angry, swarming insects in a rawhide bag, which they set out in the sun. Thus the ants were killed and dried for a highly prized sort of condiment to add to boiled meat to give it flavour.

I have mentioned that, unlike the Stoneys, the Blackfoot tribe never ate fish of any kind unless starved into it. But among us white people, the Oldman has been famous as a sport-fishing stream since away back in the 1880s. Some of the British ranchers – those same ones who introduced and organized the game of polo – had grown up angling for salmon and trout on Scottish and English rivers. It was perfectly natural for these sportsmen to angle for trout with flies fashioned from fur, tinsel, silk, and feathers, as Izaak Walton so well describes in detail in his writing. They fished no matter where they found themselves. Indeed, the old India hands had been so impressed by the rivers on the south slopes of the Himalayas that they had, with infinite difficulty, successfully introduced European brown trout to the clear, cool waters of the Kashmir, where they still flourish today.

In the Oldman they found cut-throat trout, Dolly Vardens, and Rocky Mountain whitefish, all of which will take a fly. The main river and its three forks above the Peigan Reserve must have reminded them of the rivers of their youth, though they have their own kind of beauty, with their mountain backdrops difficult to match. So when their letters home from Alberta included glowing accounts of the sport here, it isn't much wonder that keen British anglers came across the Atlantic to enjoy it. Indeed, one of these was a member of the famous Hardy family, Hardy Brothers of London, makers of the finest Tonkin cane fly rods by appointment to Their Majesties, the King and Queen. There were others who came from New York, Boston, Minneapolis, and the cities of California who revelled in the river's unsurpassed trout-fishing.

Another Englishman, and another superb fly fisherman who was drawn to the river, was Bert Riggall, who founded a professional guiding and outfitting business at Waterton Lakes in 1907. He was to become one of North America's most famous bighorn-sheep guides, with several record heads to his credit, including one killed by Martin K. Bovey (who later helped organize Trout Unlimited) that was on top of the Boone and Crockett listings for many years. He knew the wild rams of these mountains so well that he could often tell what they would do hours before they did it.

He was also a world-recognized alpine botanist, a very knowledgeable naturalist, and an amateur geologist. Apart from fall hunting, he specialized in taking families out on twenty-one- to thirty-day pack trips into the Rockies in summer, with long strings of forty or more horses. These guests enjoyed not only grand service, but a wilderness experience second to none. For Bert Riggall was more than just a professional guide, he was a very articulate man, able to explain everything seen on these trips. No man, woman, or child privileged to sit around his evening campfires listening to his stories of the country and the animals, birds, and people in it could help being deeply influenced. For he was a master raconteur, with a keen sense of humour and a photographic mind that forgot nothing of importance he ever read, heard, or saw. His guests were all wealthy, highly educated people, who could afford to go anywhere in the world, but they came again and again because they realized that this prince among mountain men was giving them something very rare. Eventually Bert found himself instructing and entertaining the grandchildren of those young adventurers that he had guided at the beginning of his career. He had made himself immortal, or as close to it as anyone ever gets.

We youngsters who grew up there at the foot of the shining mountains learned to read and do our sums in the quaint and drafty one-room schools that were scattered across the land. But we were also students in the wild and sometimes dangerous school of hard knocks close to and among the snow-capped peaks visible from our doors. And from the adult world around us we learned that to be socially successful you had to learn to tell stories. The position you held making a living or the quality of your clothing was not half as important as being able to take part in the art of story-telling. Among the cowboys, trappers, mountain men, homesteaders, and ranchers that I knew growing up, those that were good raconteurs could hold any audience enthralled. The stories from the Oldman territory alone would have filled many books. We heard about Lost Lemon Mine, the legendary gold deposit in the mountains between the Highwood and the Crowsnest Pass, found by prospectors around 1870, one of whom killed the other and then went mad. The secret location was supposed to be known to the Stoneys, but many searchers for the lost mine were believed to have died mysterious deaths. And we knew, of course, about the well-recorded deaths in the Frank Slide of 1903, when a whole town in the Crowsnest Pass was wiped out in a rock slide.

Some of us were musicians, too, who played for the local dances and concerts. No longer did the throb of Indian drums resound from tipi camps on the flats along the Oldman, but now there was lively and sometimes haunting music of a different kind marking the change of human settlement.

Like most young men eighteen years old, I entertained dreams. Sometimes they were conflicting, but they always pointed toward the wilderness of the mountains. From just about the time I was able to ride and walk, I had been "going up the creek and over the mountain" just to see what was on the other side by way of easing an itchy-footed curiosity about the country. Knowing I was looking at only the edge of a huge piece of geography full of mountains that reached west to the Pacific coast and north to the shore of the Arctic Ocean, I studied maps, many of which had blank unexplored regions where details of rivers and mountain ranges were very sketchy, with no trails and no roads. Where to start, what to do, and how to make a living doing it were questions needing atten-tion, and sometimes the very size of the problem confronting me was discouraging. But fate has a very unexpected way of intervening sometimes, as I discovered after I had turned my hand to trapping, bronco-busting, cowboying, and all of the other jobs a healthy young man in ranching country would undertake.

One day the firing-pin of my rifle broke, rendering it useless. Something had to be done about it. I heard that the only gunsmith in the country was Bert Riggall, who carried on a gun-repair and cartridge-reloading business during the off-season months of winter. So I saddled my horse and struck out down the trail towards Water-ton Lakes Park, where his ranch was located on the edge of the park along Cottonwood Creek.

From the first moment we met, I was impressed. He had a strong, quiet way with him that spoke of authority, and when I showed him my rifle, he took it into his shop and removed the broken firing-pin. Then he went to some wooden boxes stacked along the wall of his shop, where he dug around through a vast collection of parts obviously stripped from old guns. He came up with a pin to fit my rifle, and in about the time it takes to tell it my gun was back together and in perfect working order.

He then invited me to the house. He introduced me to his wife and daughter (whom I later married) and we spent a fascinating time that stretched through supper and on into the evening. The living-room of the house was lined with books and framed photographs – a warm, friendly place presided over by a man who was not only charming but a gold-mine of information. He showed me hundreds of photographs he had taken through the mountains: pictures of wildlife, camps, long strings of horses on the trail, flowers, and everything else that illustrated the life of a professional guide and outfitter. His running commentary was delightful in its detail and understanding. Before I left, I told him that if ever he needed a man who knew a little about hunting and fishing and a bit more about handling and breaking horses, I would like to have the opportunity of working on his crew. Riding home through the night I was excited about what I had seen and heard.

The months went by, then one day the following June, word came that Bert Riggall had a job for me. I spent the next ten days halter-breaking and working with sixteen head of horses. Then I helped trail about fifty head, including the green broncs, away north along the mountains to a base camp a couple of miles inside the Gap on the Oldman River. It was Bert who first told me of the pile of prayer stones; but it was recently gone when I trailed through the Gap with his horses along the newly built road, to get to know the country of the Oldman's upper reaches among the mountains.

It was the beginning of the ten intensely interesting years that I spent with Bert Riggall and his pack-train during which I came to know the cream of North American sportsmen and their families. Our camps were pitched all the way from the head of the Highwood

River to the International Border and west to the upper reaches of the North Fork of the Flathead River in British Columbia. From June to the end of August, we took summer parties fishing, climbing, and sightseeing. In September and October, we hunted the country on the heads of the Oldman and the Highwood.

Never once did I get tired of listening to Bert's endless repertoire of stories about natural history, hunting trails, and the experiences of a lifetime spent in those mountains. Never once did we exchange angry words when things went wrong and horses, rough country, and climate conspired to try the depths of our patience. Next to mules, mountain horses can be about as independent as any animal upon earth. These ones knew the country as well as the wild animals that lived there. The wrangler who rode out at daybreak to round them up soon got a first-hand knowledge of the country, for they often went for miles. Once I remember finding them at least twenty-five miles upriver from camp; they had walked most of the night to get there. That ride back through rough country on a green bronc was one to remember. It was midnight when I got them back to camp.

During the summer trips it was part of my job to guide and look after fishermen. Part of this work dealt with teaching youngsters to fly-fish for trout. The headwaters of the Oldman up there among the mountains provided ideal water for it; no matter how clumsily a fly was presented, the trout would take it, for the river was full of them. No boy or girl could possibly get bored with lack of action.

Naturally we could eat only a limited amount of fish, so it was necessary to teach these youngsters how to release the fish they caught, without injury. We were practising the catch-and-release technique long before it became evident to many people that if you wish to maintain good trout-fishing in any river, there is a limit to the number of fish that can be harvested.

Of all the people I met in those ten years with Bert Riggall, the youngsters stand out very clearly in my memory – two of them in particular. One of them was Josephine, daughter of a wealthy financier, nine years old and pretty as a dewdrop in the morning sun. She latched onto this lanky horse-wrangler, and besides being ever in my shadow, she wrapped me around her little finger.

We were camped down on the river opposite the Beehive, about which I'll talk later, and one day were preparing to ride upstream for a picnic and some fishing. She, no doubt harking back to a story about the Indians and the buffalo of past days that Bert had told the night before, asked me if we might find a buffalo skull. I told her that we had never found one in this valley, but if we did on this trip, it was hers. She gave me a lovely smile and her eyes lit up in an anticipation that was wonderful to see — even if I never expected her to get her wish.

About an hour and a half later I was leading the way across a small, dry swamp by the stream when just ahead of my horse's nose I spotted two little bones showing white against the black earth. The next moment I was down beside it digging with my belt knife in the damp, peaty earth. In a few minutes we were all standing around in utter amazement. Upside down in the damp earth, it was beautifully preserved — a buffalo skull, complete with nose bone and horn-caps. The lower jaw was gone, but all the teeth of the upper jaw were there. I had only seen one other as well preserved in my life.

Josephine stood there looking down at it and then at me with a quiet expression of wonder and confidence that shook me. She had expressed a wish, and I had fulfilled it — just as simple as that.

Picking it up, I handed it to her. "It's all yours," I told her, "but don't ask me how it happened. I'll bet I've ridden over it twenty times or more without seeing it."

Bert was quietly smiling as he helped me roll it in a piece of canvas and pack it in one of the boxes carried by the lunch horse. He knew I wanted to keep that skull so bad that I could taste it. But a promise to a child is a promise one keeps.

The experience opened up a whole new vista of the prehistoric past of this valley that I was coming to know so well. I had seen and examined the great reef of solid oyster-shell on the head of Oyster Creek, which was millions of years old, but the buffalo skull came from about two hundred years ago, from the time the great herds had grazed here. It was a much nearer and warmer part of the history of this wild valley.

Another summer, young Bob, one of Bert's grandsons, came with us. He was a wiry, happy-go-lucky urchin with a pixie grin who rode as if he had been born on horseback. We jokingly called him Packrat because he was always picking up things wherever he went, and had an especially keen eye for Indian artifacts. It seemed he could smell them, for in a very few days he uncovered two sites that had obviously been used by flint-knappers, as the scores of chips of chert and some arrowheads revealed. It did not seem to matter where we went, he was always picking up evidence of Stone Age Indians.

Late one evening, when it was almost dark, he and I were bringing the horses to camp. He was riding at a trot just ahead of me when he came off his horse as if he had been shot. Reaching down, he picked something up out of the trail dust, grinned happily, and handed it to me. It was a fine stone arrowhead, which I had previously ridden over countless times in full daylight, without seeing it. Bob quite often made me feel as though I was blind, since he truly had the gift of looking and being able to see. He also contributed to my awareness of the people who had been along the Oldman before us.

Those headwaters of the Oldman were always fascinating. Here the creeks were like the branches at the top of a tree, short but numerous little streams that flowed down out of basins along the front of the Continental Divide, from among the folds of some lovely natural timberline parks and high passes. There was the Beehive, Tornado Peak, and Gould's Dome to name a few of the higher mountains – all between nine and ten thousand feet above sea level at their summits.

In summer we often took climbing parties up the Beehive, which was absolutely sheer on its north face, but much easier along the ridge at its back. From its peak, the view reached for hundreds of miles in every direction; we could see the Kootenay country in British Columbia to the west, the high mountains up along the Athabasca to the north, and away south to the Divide in Montana. Following down the Oldman to the east, we could see the far rim of the prairie, blue in the distance overtop the Livingstone Range near the Gap.

The Beehive is more than just a prominent peak; it was the spiritual home of the Old Man in the eyes of the Blackfoot people. As we stood there on the peak, it was not hard to imagine why. At our feet were dozens of old and new lightning pits, craters blasted out of solid rock big enough to sit in, for this mountain is a natural lightning-rod. Safe in our camps in the valley we often watched the lightning play on it during thunderstorms – nature's great, awesome pyrotechnical displays. It is doubtful if any Blackfoot ever climbed it, for they were never mountaineers; but if any of the bolder warriors did, they must have been filled with a feeling of being very close to the Great Spirit, as we were.

Back then it was great game country, with bighorns, mountain goats, mule deer, elk, moose, black bears, and grizzlies. Late one August, Bert and I were out on a pre-hunting-season scouting trip when we walked upon a limestone outcrop overlooking a salt-lick on the edge of a big basin drained by Soda Creek. Without moving, we were able to count close to forty big mule-deer bucks, some of them with wide, heavy racks still in velvet. Back of them, among the broken cliffs, a round dozen bighorn rams lazed in their beds pawed deep in the loose talus. Then my binoculars picked up a black speck wheeling against the blue sky far above the Beehive to our right – a golden eagle. It suddenly peeled off the edge of a cloud to come down in a sizzling dive across the face of the peak. Down it came, into a patch of shintangle on the crest of a low ridge at our level about half a mile away. What it struck there, only the eagle knew, but its descent was an unforgettable piece of drama synonymous with the wilderness.

Two of the creeks flowing into the Oldman from the north had colourful names: Slacker and Profanity. As you would expect, there were stories back of them.

During the First World War, a compulsory draft law was passed in Canada to gather up men who were not volunteering. Four or five young cowboys from the ranching country east of the mountains decided they were going into hiding, so they saddled up and headed into the high country with a string of pack-horses. It was late fall, with snow on the ground, and they did not know the trails, but they headed out through the mountains to the west, determined to put some distance behind them. They were getting close to the Divide when they came up on a high ridge and headed down a creek flowing to the southwest. There they found a secluded pocket in the timber and made camp. They built a log cabin and turned their horses loose to go back to their home range. Ironically, without knowing it, they had built their cabin within a mile of the old Indian trail leading up the Oldman.

No doubt the winter went by slowly, for they had little to do except some hunting limited by deep snow, not to mention cutting firewood and playing cards. When spring finally came, it was very welcome. All but one of them decided that the army was better than this, so they headed toward home. The remaining slacker finally made his way on into the United States, where he waited out the war on a remote ranch in Washington State. He, it turned out, was also the lone survivor. The walls of their old cabin are still standing today on Slacker Creek.

After the First World War, the Forestry Department had the bright idea of hiring some recently demobilized fighter pilots to patrol the mountain country on lookout for fires. They flew little single-engine biplanes left over from the war. As a prerequisite exercise to qualify for their jobs, they were required to ride over some of the country they would be seeing from the air, to orient themselves with it. For some of them with city backgrounds, this was to be a difficult experience.

A small party of these pilots once rode up the Oldman inside the Gap, following the trail above the forks along the Livingstone River. They swung west up a Forestry trail on Savannah Creek that led them up onto the same ridge that the slackers had found. Here they paused to contemplate the geography and check their maps. They knew that a camp awaited their arrival down at the falls of the Oldman to the southeast. The trail they were following went west for several miles to Oyster Creek, where they would double back toward camp. Sore muscles from hours of riding begrudged this extra distance, so they decided to cheat and shortcut down the first creek straight for the river.

What was a matter of only about three miles on the map resolved itself into a nightmare of down timber and thick brush, requiring axe-work for every yard of progress. In desperation they rode into the creek and followed it, only to find themselves cut off by a perpendicular falls in the bottom of a steep-sided canyon. By the time they had backtracked out of this trap, it was dark, and they had to spend a miserable night in the bush with no blankets or food, and lots of mosquitoes for company. When they staggered into camp next day, they knew for sure that what looks like a shortcut in the mountains can be the long way around. Up to that point, the creek that they had followed and the high ridge behind it had no names on the map. They, with good reason, pencilled in Profanity Creek and Profanity Range, names that, along with Slacker Creek, became official. Until very recently, that is, when some bureaucrat who knew nothing of the stories behind them changed them to some colourless substitutes with no history behind them.

10 *People Along the River*

From the home ranch near Waterton Park to our base camp on Racehorse Creek inside the Gap was about ninety miles. We made an average of two round trips a season trailing forty-odd head of loose horses. It was a two-day ride each way, which took us across a number of tributaries of the Oldman, just a few miles east of the mountains. At first there were two of us making the trip, but later I persuaded Bert that I could trail the bunch alone, for I liked the work and knew the country well enough to make it easy. When a bunch of horses become accustomed to one man, they handle even better than with two riders. A lone rider doesn't get his concentration sidetracked, and can better anticipate problems before they happen.

Well into the shank of an afternoon one long, hot day, I was heading south up out of the Crowsnest River valley past a bench inside a rancher's field. There was an open gate leading to the field, and perhaps hoping I would stop and camp for the night, the leaders of the bunch trotted through it and fanned out to feed. I was riding around to haze them back out onto the road when I suddenly noticed an old hidden tipi ring of stones, which the Indians had used to hold their tents down in this windy country. I soon found that it was only one of about a hundred such rings on the bench, and they had been there a long time, for many of the rocks, six to eight inches through, were barely showing in the sod, and it takes a lot of years for sod to build up around surface rocks of this size. Sitting there on my horse, it was easy to visualize the big camp that was once pitched here with probably three to four hundred people. Old buffalo-hunters, these ones, people who had ranged up and down this valley before there were any white people.

It was not the first time that I had found tipi rings along these rivers, nor would it be the last. But it was always a thrill, like riding into a historic review of the past, when this was all unfenced, open country with buffalo dotting the hills on an ocean of grass running far beyond the horizon, and halfway across the continent. It was something to think about as the horses jogged on south toward the Castle a few miles farther.

It was evening when I came down to the river, the horses spreading out at the near edge of the shallow crossing to drink. For some reason known only to herself, old Cee-Cee, the lead mare, turned upstream instead of heading into the river and led the bunch under a steep bank. I rode up along the top of it to head her off and stepped my horse out near its edge to yell at her and turn her back. Immediately I smelled smoke and to my amazement saw a stovepipe sticking out of the ground almost under my left stirrup. At the same time a voice down below yelled, "Get the hell off the roof, before you come through!" My horse jumped sideways just as a man appeared on a little shelf a few feet down the bank against a clump of willows.

My surprise was complete as I sat there on my horse looking at him. He was of medium height and indeterminate age, with a face as brown and wrinkled as a sun-cured prune and a pair of eyes that were clear blue and sharp.

"Seeing as how you rode out on my roof, you might as well get down and come in, Russell," he said with a grin. "I've seen you cross down below with that string of broomtails often enough to know who you are."

I stepped down, and picked up a rock to shy ahead of old Cee-Cee with a yell to go with it. She plunged into the river and headed across. The idea of a cool swim must have seemed like a good one, for the whole bunch followed her across, including the pack-horse. My sleeping-bag was on top of the pack and out of the water, which was a comfort.

Climbing down to where my unexpected host was standing, I grinned at him and shook his hand. Although I had not seen him since I was half-grown, I knew who he was. For Bill was something of a legend; hunter, trapper, cowboy when he felt like it, and on occasion there were rumours that he was a moonshiner. He was a crack rifle-shot and spent a large part of every winter ranging far and wide across the hills hunting coyotes for their skins.

"Got a nice bull trout this afternoon," he told me. "It's about suppertime. When you get your camp set up, better come and have a bait."

I accepted his invitation and went back to my horse and rode back down to the crossing. By the time I had caught and saddled a fresh horse and spread my bed under a tree, the sun had dipped behind the hills. Riding back across the river, I hobbled my horse on a little meadow among some aspens and climbed down to Bill's dugout. The door stood open and Bill was busy at the stove. The inside of the place was neat and the walls and roof were lined with old weathered rough planks that looked as if they had once been the flooring of a bridge. They were supported by a log centre beam and two side beams, each of which were held up by three stout posts. The stock of a rifle peeped out of a buckskin case hung on two pegs set into one of the beams, and a miscellany of equipment was tucked under the bunk at the back of the dugout. The table was a couple of wide boards on two oak barrels, and on the well-swept board floor a row of stone crocks stood along the base of one wall with a coil of copper tubing over them.

When I had washed off the dust in a wash-basin on a shelf outside the door, Bill poured a measure of clear liquid out of a jug into a cup and handed it to me.

"Sample some of my white mule to celebrate," he said, "seeing as how you're the first to ride on my roof."

He poured some for himself in another cup, and by way of a toast he laughed and said, "Here's to your ornery old pack-horses and mud in your eye!" whereupon he downed it in one gulp.

I took a sip and almost choked, for that so-called white mule had a kick like one – pure liquid fire.

"Don't be scared of it," Bill grinned, "it's pure stuff filtered in charcoal to take out the gook. Make the hair grow on your chest!"

I took another cautious sip and thought it would more likely burn the hair off.

We had a good supper of fresh fried trout, Dutch-oven biscuits, and boiled new potatoes, topped off with canned peaches, which we ate off our knees as we squatted outside where it was cool. Then we lit up smokes and sat back to trade some stories.

That was a fascinating evening, for Bill was in an unusually loquacious mood. He told me about riding north to Canada from the States many years before through this country along the Old-man – a fugitive from a gunfight with a rancher who had some vengeful relatives.

"I kept right on going to hell and gone beyond, away north into British Columbia. Figured on staying there, but it wasn't in the cards. I remembered this country and came back. Been here ever since."

He had a real love for this mountain and foothill country and knew the river from its headwaters to away down on the prairie. Like me he had come to know it and to love the spirit of its movement through feeling the push of it against his legs. We had both fished it, and trapped beaver up along the creeks in spring. We could talk about it, though there was no need. Like the Indians, we had looked and learned something about how to really see and feel its power. Like the smell of campfires burning under a starry sky, or the whispering and roaring of the wind in the trees and among the high rocks, it was something we shared in our blood.

Bill told me that, more out of the challenge of it than anything else, he had been making the odd batch of "white mule" on and off for several years. He had been careful where he sold it, going far enough away so his still wouldn't be easy to find. When he had dug out this place, he had planted the willows outside to hide the front of it. In winter the snow drifted down deep over it; he had a log cabin further up the Castle, where he lived most of the time.

"But lately," he told me, "I been having bad dreams about windows with bars on them, and wake up in a cold sweat. Reckon a couple of close shaves with the Mounties started it. Got a feeling that landing in jail would kill me. I been free as the mountains for too long. If you had come a couple of days later, this would be only a hole in the ground. I'm quittin' while the quittin' is good!"

When I rode down the trail toward the home ranch the next morning, I knew I had met a real character. Bill lived for more years after that visit, enjoying the mountain trails, and with no more bad dreams about bars on windows.

There are few straight lines in the designs of nature: almost everything about it is a combination of interwoven curves, subtle sweeping outlines of form and motion. Some are obvious and some are hidden, and the understanding takes time. A river is the ultimate proof of it, for the water lifts and eddies, swirls and curls back on itself, jumps and falls in a myriad of interwoven patterns so simple and yet complex. This complexity will always be a real challenge to a fisherman presenting a tiny lure of fur, feathers, silk, or tinsel, so that it will drift naturally without dragging and giving itself away for the fraud that it is. The skill involved with fly fishing makes it an art, and sometimes an exasperation. It is not enough to tie the fly so that it closely resembles the insect on which the trout is feeding; the good fisherman must present it with sufficient skill and delicacy to make it irresistibly attractive to the fish. The eyes of a trout are sharp and discerning, and really big ones do not get that way by being careless.

It is not necessary to be a fly fisherman to truly love a river, but it helps. This love of rivers and the pursuit of trout has shaped and moulded some very special characters I met along the river.

There is Bob, who first came to know the Oldman while courting a rancher's daughter, with his mind on things other than fish. It took some time and concentration to persuade the girl that life with him would be utter bliss, during which he somehow did not elaborate unduly on the fact that at times she would be a fisherman's and hunter's widow. She, being a smart girl, no doubt knew this already, and loved him anyway.

For a while Bob gallantly ignored the river, but one fine summer day they went on a picnic at a spot overlooking a pool, where they sat in the warm sun and wove dreams for a while, blind to everything but each other. Suddenly the quiet of the afternoon brought the unmistakable slurping sound of the rise of a big trout to his ears. He was suddenly totally alert, like a pointer dog with a noseful of the scent of grouse. A minute or two went by before that slurping sound came again, and this time he turned to see the rise beside a half-sunken driftwood log sticking out from the bank sixty feet or so up on the far side of the pool. Mumbling something, he rushed to the car parked near by and extracted from its trunk a cased rod and a fishing-vest with numerous pockets well stuffed with various things. With deft fingers he put the rod together, fitted his reel to its handle, strung the line through the guides, and then carefully tied a fly – a Letort Hopper – to the tippet of the leader. Without the slightest thought for his polished shoes or the sport slacks he was wearing, he went to the edge of the pool and waded out into the shallows at its tail until he was thigh-deep and directly below the end of the log. With consummate skill he worked out line with two or three false casts, at the same time stripping a bit more from the reel which he held in a loop with his left hand. Without breaking the rhythm of the rod, he gracefully shot the fly upstream, dropping it with delicacy and precision on top of the log. The gentle drag of the river on the line nudged the fly off the log into the water, where it floated with saucy daring on the surface directly over the trout's lair.

There was a quick swirl and Bob lifted the rod tip with a firm hand. A heavy rainbow trout exploded out of the water, fell back, and then came out again to tail-walk in a shower of spray before falling back to bore down toward the log. Bob did not yell – he is not the yelling kind – but he turned the fish out into the pool, where the dancing rod and the screaming reel told the story of its wild efforts to throw the tiny hook in its jaw. After a dramatic few minutes, Bob slowly backed out to the edge of the gravel bar, finally leading the tired fish to his feet. Stooping, he caught it by the gills and lifted it triumphantly out of the water.

Remembering that he had company, and with due regard for the girl's sensitivity, he turned his back to give the trout the coup de grâce on the head with a rock. He then carried it to her in triumph, and she, with shining eyes expressing admiration for his skill and daring, proceeded to throw her arms around his neck and give him a kiss of some duration. It was later that he became aware for the first time that he had forgotten to put on his waders.

Bob is a lawyer, and a bit of an eccentric, though inclined to dress in conservatively traditional pinstripe suits in his office. On the stream, he generally resembles a dignified bum, wearing clothes that are well marked by service, topped by a disreputable fly-strewn hat that looks as if it had been trampled by a herd of stampeding buffalo. He takes his fly fishing and hunting just as seriously as his law, but tempers it by writing delightful stories and articles about it. He purely loves the Oldman and regularly abandons his office to go fishing there at every opportunity. One can imagine his secretary answering a call at such times.

"Sorry, sir, but he is not in the office today. Where can he be reached? By four-wheel drive and waders somewhere in the Oldman River, I believe. It's trout season you know."

After a lot of years, he is still married to the same woman, which says something.

One summer a few years back, Bob was fishing the Oldman near the forks when he came upon a boy about twelve years old sitting by the sawed-off stump of a big driftwood red-fir log. He was carefully counting the annual rings of the tree on the bevelled butt of the stump, which had been smoothed with a razor-sharp axe to reveal them. Filled with curiosity, Bob introduced himself and the boy gave his name as Rob.

"That's short for Robert, the same as mine," Bob told him and then asked about the log.

"Grandpa and I found it. It was washed down here on last spring's flood, I guess. He cut two gateposts off it. He thought it would be good if I counted the rings and found out how old it is. He says this big stump is about the best history book there is. I guess he's right. I've been having trouble with history at school."

"How's it going?" Bob asked.

"Pretty slow," Rob told him. "The rings are awful close together in some places. Grandpa says those are the dry years. See these ones here," and he pointed to some very fine rings not far under the bark. "Those are the dry years in the 'hungry thirties'." Then he pointed to a dark ring farther down. "This was when a fire went through, burning the grass and brush."

He went on to explain how fir trees have thick bark resistant to fire and how it doesn't kill the tree unless it gets up into the green needles among the branches. "Grandpa says little fires on the ground are good for fir trees. They keep the brush down so flames don't get high enough to burn the top of the trees."

He had marked certain rings with a sharp pencil and noted dates. "This one I marked is 1905. That's when Alberta became a province. This one here is 1874 when the Mounted Police came and built Fort Macleod down the river. Here's 1877. That's when they signed the treaty with the Indians." Then he pointed positively to another ring: "This one is 1753. That's the year Anthony Henday came two hundred and seventeen years ago. He was the first white man to see the mountains. That's the last date in my book about this country. I guess I'll have to go back in Canada's history before 1753 now."

Bob could remember the dismally boring history books of his early school years. This boy had a smart grandfather who had seen a way to bring history alive for him, and at the same time open up an inquiring mind. As much as Bob had been around, up and down the rivers from the Red Deer River south to here, this was the first time he had really seen a tree right down to its heart. He asked how old this one was.

The boy pondered for a while. "I guess I won't know for sure till I count all the rings. But it will be easier towards the middle. You see, the rings are farther apart there. Trees like this grow faster when they are younger. But it must be close to eight hundred years."

"That will take you back into European history," Bob said. "Look, Rob, I've got a chain-saw in my Scout back about half a mile, and I think we can cut off this bevelled piece. It's too heavy to carry very far, but we can put it in the river and float it down to the car. Then we'll take it down to your place, for you to show at school. And I'd like to meet your grandfather and your parents."

It was mid-afternoon by the time Bob got back with the saw and cut off the required section of the stump. In the meantime, the boy had stripped down to his shorts and sneakers. They launched the awkward piece of wood into the river and Rob went with it, swimming with the smoothness of an otter in the deep places and pushing it along in the shallows. When it got stuck, Bob waded in to help him wrestle it free.

"This is the way Grandpa got the posts down," Rob said, "only he used his horse and rope. They were awful heavy. Kept getting hung up. Made ol' Baldy snort." He chuckled, then, "Grandpa cussed when he broke his rope."

When they loaded the piece of log into Bob's vehicle, and drove down to the ranch buildings along a twisted trail, the two thick posts were standing upright on each side of the driveway entrance in freshly dug holes. Rob's father and grandfather were there and the boy introduced them.

"I started out fishing today, but I got sidetracked in history," Bob told them. "This boy has been teaching me something I've never thought about before."

Bob had supper with the family, and when he drove to his father-in-law's ranch later, he knew that sometimes there is a lot more to fishing than just catching fish.

Joe shares the river with us. Like me, he was born and grew up on one of its tributaries, learning how to survive in the Rocky Mountain school of hard knocks while coming to feel the spirits of the wilderness and its rivers. A fly fisherman by choice and a mechanic and truck-driver by vocation, he is a big, lean man with rugged features, a sunny disposition, and wonderful skill. Whether he is handling heavy tools on some oilwell drilling-site or plying his fly rod on some stream, his love for his work and play shines. He knows the Oldman up, down, around, and through probably better than any man alive.

Graduating from chucking bait with a willow pole to a steel rod and then to a fly rod, he learned to tie his own flies with whatever fur and feathers came to hand, an exercise that moved in his case from skill to sheer artistry. Joe knows a lot about the insect life in the river, a talent that does not run to Latin terminology but is none the less astonishingly well informed. He is always questing and experimenting; and, not being able to afford the kind of tackle he wanted, he began to make his own rods.

Joe is strong as a bear, with the big muscular hands that go with it, and it is purely amazing to watch the delicacy exercised in his making of a fine-tuned fly rod. Not a wrap of silk is a hundredth of an inch out of place, the guides are properly spaced for maximum shooting of the line, and the cork handle is shaped and dressed to fit the hand. When he has it set up to meet his critical eye and it has met the necessary balance with the chosen weight of line by way of some testing on the lawn of his backyard, he signs it "Joe Cutch" (a simplified version of his real name, which is as Italian as the Tiber River) at the base of the shaft just above the grip. After another coat of varnish, it is ready for the customer. Anyone lucky enough to own one of his rods knows that he or she has the best available, finely balanced and strong.

Regardless of where it flows on the face of the earth, a river is always the lifeblood of the surrounding country. A river with its valley is one of nature's greatest architectural designs of power and beauty; a living drama in which man struggles towards perfect adjustment with his environment. The Oldman is just one river among many, but none the less is vital to those who live along its course – a river with a long history, unique in its unspoiled wildness.

A few of the ranchers living along the river understood this and valued the Oldman highly. But to many of them, it was just handy water flowing past their homesteads, water to be used for irrigation of gardens and crops, and for drinking. When bad sewage-disposal practices of towns in Crowsnest Pass on the middle fork rendered it unfit for drinking, people downstream resorted to wells and springs without complaint.

For the most part, they took the river for granted. It was here, it was always here, and it would always be here. In summer the murmur of its flow lulled those who lived close to it to sleep. They heard it, but did not really hear its message, just as they looked at it every day and did not really see it. It was a fixture, unchanging except for occasional floods that came over its banks. Sometimes the ice went out at spring break-up time with a sudden booming roar. Then there could be dangerous ice-jams that caused damage to property, and these left miniature stranded icebergs weeping in the sun till they disappeared. But for the rest of the year it was the river, the Oldman, a wandering crooked line on the map. Very few of the ranchers knew or cared that it was the holy river of the Blackfoot people. Many of them had picked the stones of tipi rings off their fields, a nuisance to be rid of.

But then there came a rumour of a dam to be built a few miles downstream below the forks near Pincher Creek, and those who lived in the valleys became worried. We knew that a possible site had been surveyed years before, but many such sites had been abandoned as unfeasible. Two dams had been built, one on the Waterton River a few miles downstream from the park and the other on the St. Mary's River just below the town of Cardston. Both rivers are important tributaries of the Oldman and were excellent trout streams, and both dams had flooded thousands of acres of good land.

About the time of the first rumours, I spent a day with my fly rod on the North Fork of the Oldman, a mile or so above where it joins the Castle and the Crowsnest. In early afternoon, I left the stream to sit with my back to a big cottonwood, taking time out from fishing for some lunch and a pipe. It was a lovely day, with a gentle breeze and a few clouds running overhead. I was close to being asleep when across the river I saw a girl riding a pinto pony bareback with a guitar slung across her back. When she came opposite, she angled away to a clump of trees where she dismounted to tie up her horse. Then she took the guitar up the steep slope to a sandstone outcrop where she sat down on a ledge. For a while she remained motionless, looking up the river. Then she began to strum the strings and broke into song. It was too far away for me to hear the words, but it was an enchanting melody I had never heard before – a lovely addition to a perfect afternoon. Then a feeling came to me that I was intruding, so I moved away through the trees, back toward a spot where a good trout had missed my fly earlier in the day.

Wading out into the pool where the big trout lay, I stood watching for a while, the gentle current cool against my legs. Hundreds of stonefly nymphs were crawling up onto stones projecting out of the water above the pool, shucking their skins and drying their wings before taking to the air. Some of the big flat-winged insects were falling off the rocks into the water, others were landing on various plants along the river to gather strength before taking wing again on their egg-laying runs over the surface. This was the final stage of a three-year cycle, a moment fly fishermen dream about, when trout go into a feeding frenzy beyond anything like the normal. Some of the inch-long insects were even landing on me as I selected a stiff hackled bucktail replica from my fly box and tied it to the tippet of my leader.

A good trout rolled to one side of a boulder farther up the pool. Dropping the fly a bit upstream and slightly to one side of the spot, I watched it floating down in company with a live specimen, and knew a thrill of excitement when the trout took the artificial fly in a solid strike. It came out of the water in a cart-wheeling leap, bored down deep behind the rock, jumped again, and then shot way across the pool. It was a thick-bodied, handsome rainbow, iridescent in the sun as it jumped again and again. When it finally submitted to being led down into the shallow water, I slipped the hook out of its jaw and watched it go swimming back to deep water.

The next hour was one of the wildest, most action-packed sessions I have ever spent. I used up more time cleaning and drying my fly than I did fishing, for the trout took it with reckless abandon almost every cast. When one got chewed beyond recognition or ability to float, I put on another, and the unbridled feeding went on. I lost count of the fish played and released. I tried every trick cast and type of fly presentation I knew, and the trout kept striking.

Finally I worked my way down to a big pool where the river split itself on a huge boulder shaped like a Gothic church door sticking up a good three feet out of deep water. On my side there was a gravel bar and on the other a low undercut bank with a big willow overhanging it. For a while I just stood watching.

The stonefly hatch was slowing up, but the trout were still rising steadily. A couple of good ones were rolling a bit below and on each side of the boulder. Then, out of the corner of my eye, I saw a gentle, slow-rolling confident rise under the willow and against the bank. There was something about that lazy rise that spoke of a grand fish. But it was in a very difficult place to reach, for if the fly did not get hung up in the willow, it would be hard to drop it where it wouldn't drag and drown on the edge of an eddy. Big trout are shy of a dragging fly, and this one had to be sophisticated in the art of survival.

Tying on a fresh leader and a new fly, I waded slowly out into the pool downstream and across from the willow until the water was threatening the top of my chest waders. Working the line out in false casts, I shot the fly with all the power in my rod in a long cast that barely missed the willow, so that it danced on the far edge of a bulge in the slow current and floated jauntily to within six inches of the bank. Then it disappeared in a tiny rise no bigger than one made by a small fish. Muttering something smoky under my breath, I struck anyway – and the water flew in every direction as a massive rainbow came out of the river in a jump that came within a whisker of fouling the leader on a low-hanging branch. It shot out into the river toward the boulder and blew the river open again with another end-swapping jump. Then followed a move that took me completely by surprise, for the trout charged straight at me quicker than I could take up the slack and jumped again close enough to splash water over me.

For a long moment I thought it was all over, but then the slack came out of the line and I could feel the weight of the fish as it made a long run downstream with the reel howling in protest. As I backed out on the edge of the gravel bar, the trout slowly swam back upstream a way and then just stopped and hung there – dead weight. I manoeuvred down to a point a bit below and across from it and it must have seen me, for it suddenly shot back up the river. Finally, after several short runs, as it began to tire, I worked it up to my feet in shallow water, where I could see every detail showing against the coloured stones on the bottom. Keeping its head toward me, I slipped my fingers under one of its gill-covers and lifted it up to admire it. It was by far the finest fish of the day and one of the finest rainbows I had seen in a lot of years of fishing along the front of the mountains.

I was about to slip the fly out of its jaw and release it when a voice behind me said, "Don't you like to eat them?"

Startled, I looked around to find an audience – the girl with the guitar sitting on her pinto horse with her long blonde hair hanging down her back and a quizzical little smile on her face.

"For sure," said, "but I kept all I wanted back up the river. Would you like this one?"

"Oh, yes!" she said, "I'll take it back to the ranch where I'm staying. They'll love to have it."

That is how I met Lesley. She was staying with some friends on a ranch farther down the river. I dressed the trout and hung it on a forked willow stick. When I handed it up to her, I noticed a shadow cross her face and asked her if something was wrong.

"I've heard about the dam," she said. "I just can't believe anyone would drown this beautiful valley. All this will be under water, my friends say, and they will lose their ranch. Isn't there something that can be done to stop it?" She was near tears.

"So far, it's only a rumour," I told her. "But if it gets serious, some of us are sure going to try."

11 *The Death of the River?*

It soon became very evident that the rumour was fact. In 1976 the government announced that it was planning to dam the Oldman just a few miles below the confluence of the three forks of the river where it ran through a canyon. The lake thus formed would flood all three valleys and drown thirty-one ranches to a greater or lesser extent, making all of them uneconomic, and completely destroying the home sites of nearly every one of the parcels of land involved. Some of the old homes date back to before the turn of the century, qualifying them as historic sites in the early settlement of the country by the old-time cattle-ranchers.

To those of us who know something of the impact of dams, culturally, environmentally, and ecologically, the announcement of the planned dam was a catastrophe. We knew that these features of the issue would likely be totally ignored in the rush to provide big construction contracts, lots of (temporary) construction jobs, and irrigation water to relatively few farmers. We were aware that the economics of the proposal would include as costs only the actual construction of the dam and the expenses involved with the appropriation of the lands due to be inundated. For the history of such projects here or anywhere else on the continent, or in the world, shows that the cost estimates never include all the damage done to the people who really own the rivers – and pay for their destruction, in every way.

I wondered what the Peigan people living on their reserve a few miles further downstream would think of such a development, which not only would interfere with the holy river of the Blackfoot tribes but would also affect their lands. For if water was to be used to irrigate farmlands to the east, it had to be taken by canal down through the property granted to the Peigans by long-standing treaty rights. They had been hosts to water diversion for irrigation use north of the river from a weir and a canal located on their land since 1910. How would they react to this additional intrusion? The government proposal, which involved hundreds of pages of information (and what turned out to be considerable disinformation), made no mention of how much land would be needed for this canal, or what arrangements had been made with the Peigans for its use.

No part of the report made any mention of whether the formations of the land and the underlying bedrock would, literally, hold water. Those of us who had been interested enough to look at it over the years knew that the bedrock was extremely porous sandstone with overlying beds of gravel, sand, and what appeared to be some layers of volcanic ash here and there. All of this is about as water-proof as a sponge. When the dam-site surveyors had drilled down into the formations on both sides of the river several years before, the porous nature of the sandstone had forced them to use compressed air to keep the drilling bits clear; when water was injected under normal procedures it just kept right on going into the rock.

All of this made it unlikely that the proposed holding-basin could even be filled with water unless its whole bottom was lined with concrete. With canyons running in from both sides, overhanging cliffs here and there all along the river on its tributaries, and the generally steep topography of most of the slopes, this would be an astronomically expensive undertaking, if not totally impossible. To make matters worse, the slopes of the valley are prone to sluffing – and such massive landslides into the water would be accentuated by flooding. Not only is sluffing very damaging to the holding potential of water in such a lake, but it can be downright dangerous to a dam, drastically altering its topography, or its level.

I had travelled back and forth across this land on foot, on horseback, and by automobile for years, and the memory of seeing it from the ground made me wonder about something. So I chartered a light plane and flew over it. From a height of three thousand feet, the whole area was laid out like a map — every detail of the rivers I had fished so often, every home site and their relation to the land in sharp detail. In a few minutes we could travel across country that had once taken me all day on saddle-horse. We winged out over the lower stretch of the Castle, banked north to the Crowsnest, and followed it up to where we could see it come out at the mountains like a silver rope cast in sinuous curves along its valley between the hills. Then we swung north, flying parallel to the front of the long ridge of the Livingstone Range, across the Todd Creek valley, and over onto the North Fork of the Oldman a few miles downriver from the Gap. It was a crystal-clear day as we winged back down the Oldman with the great grassy basin of the Waldron Ranch off our larboard wing, the front of the Porcupine Hills dead ahead, and the sweep of farming and ranching land to starboard. Following the river we could see every fold of the ground as we flew back to the dam site, and I knew that what I had suspected was true. In all of that great expanse of country there was not one lake or slough, apart from some beaver ponds along Todd Creek. Unlike the country a few miles to the south, which is dotted with lakes and sloughs, this area was like blotting-paper: its porous, sandy soil soaked up the run-off water and would not hold it.

I wondered if the Minister of Lands and Forests or any of his immediate advisers had ever flown over it, or, if they had, if they could understand what they had seen.

Another pass with the plane took us high up along the east front of the Continental Divide, from Waterton Park in the south,

following the main range of the Rockies north. From the headwaters of the South Branch of the Castle River on the park border
through to the head of Oyster Creek, we flew over country that I
had travelled for twenty-five years with the pack-train, when it was
so wild that the only trails were those we had cut or that had been
blazed through virgin forests by the Stoney Indians. This was the
core of the Oldman, the area where its many branches flowed down
off the roof-tree of the continent through twisted canyons and across
flower-strewn green meadows. I had often seen animals there – elk,
deer, moose, bighorn sheep, mountain goats, bears, and others –
thousands of them over the years, but it had never occurred to me
that the most powerful and numerous of them all could possibly do
as much damage in so short a time.

The tracks of man showed here now. The heavy scars of roads –
for logging and for oil and gas exploration – were traced along every
river and almost every creek on the east slope of the Rockies. And,
what was much worse, the timber at the headwaters among the
high timberline basins was being clear-cut, leaving thousands of
acres of naked slopes criss-crossed with the tracks of heavy machines
and the smashed remnants of shattered trees wasted in the rush for
profit where there really was none. With all cover ruthlessly ripped
away, the topsoil, the vital and precious resource that had been
slowly accumulating for 10,000 years since the Ice Age had melted
off these mountains, was now being washed away downhill in
spring run-offs that carried it in brown floods down the river.

What was incongruous and contradictory about this was that if
the dam was being built to control floods – as we had been told by
government news releases to the press – why was this problem being
exacerbated by cutting timber in the river basin that was its natural
control, and why did the government continue to hand out clear-
cutting licences?

I had flown down the length of the Mediterranean over country
where people first realized the power and fertility of the soil many

thousands of years ago. They had multiplied there, built great cities, and known enormous wealth. They had cleared the forests then flourishing in North Africa and turned the country along the lower stretches of the Nile and in Libya into a vast granary. They had cut the cedars and other trees on the beautiful areas of Lebanon and Crete for timber and masts for their ships to carry them afar on voyages of conquest and trade. When the timber was gone, they had turned loose flocks of sheep and goats to eat the grass that grew to take its place. In time there was nothing to hold the rich topsoil, nine to eleven feet deep, and wind and rain had moved it down into the sea, leaving little but sand and bare rock. As a result, many of their cities had been left abandoned, while the farmlands in North Africa were claimed by encroaching desert – the Sahara – all except a narrow strip along the Nile River.

The Nile itself tells us a further instructive story. Every year floods came down this great river bringing millions of tons of natural fertilizer from up along its tropical headwaters, to flood and enrich its valley and estuary and help sustain a great fishery off the coast. The people flourished. But then, following the Second World War, the Egyptian government saw an opportunity to harness the Nile for electrical power and irrigation, and in due course negotiated a contract with Russian engineers to construct a dam. So the great Aswan Dam was built, and for a little while it seemed to be a marvellous thing.

But, as is the way with dams, nothing worked out the way the planners expected. Now that the natural fertilizers no longer come downstream, it is necessary to use artificial fertilizer and chemical insecticides, and this, along with the salinization that accompanies irrigation, is poisoning the soil more and more every year. The Nile no longer deposits vast quantities of fertile silt on surrounding land, which for thousands of years afforded good growing conditions for plants. With no replacing silt, the bed of the Nile is eroding and the banks are crumbling, while the sea relentlessly chews away at the coastline, thus reducing the estuary. Large numbers of big buildings are in danger of collapsing through instability caused by the rising water-table, while the proliferation of weeds in the irrigation canals and in the river itself is much greater than expected. As for the commercial fishing at the mouth of the Nile, that has almost disappeared.

The dam that sounded so wonderful has proved to be such a total disaster that the President of the Egyptian Republic recently appealed to scientists to put their wisdom and knowledge at the disposal of the state to solve that country's present difficulties. He pleaded, "You must help us achieve a victory over the major challenges that Egypt will have to face between now and the year 2000. What is required is a serious scientific study of all aspects of our problems, both present and future. Among these, *the secondary effects of the building of the Aswan Dam require your special attention. To overcome them is, in effect, one of the main challenges Egypt has to face.*" (my italics.)

Dams are a relatively new development in the industrial and agricultural worlds. Here in Alberta we have been aware of some of their implications since the 1960s, when the government came up with a grandiose scheme to move water south from the Mackenzie River drainage system through a complicated series of dams, diversions, and canals involving every river south to the International Border. It was called the Prime Plan, and folders expounding its advantages were circulated by mail to every taxpayer in the province. The cost of the scheme ran into billions of dollars, but the dollars then flowing into the government coffers from oil and gas development left the politicians unconcerned about the cost. But those of us who were aware of the ecological and social impacts of moving water from one river system to another, and of the enormous amount of good land that was being flooded – and of the obvious, though unmentioned, intention of eventually exporting it over the border into the United States – were deeply concerned. We knew that, as the Americans ran out of water, pressure would increase on Canadians to send their water south. As Michael Keating says in his book *To the Last Drop: Canada and the World's Water Crisis*, this would mean "turning the prairie rivers into a gigantic plumbing system".

We had plenty to be concerned about, for we had seen how brutally oil and gas exploration had been carried out on the east slope of the Rockies, and had seen the roughshod treatment handed out to private landowners with surface rights. It was perfectly obvious we were all up against a get-rich-quick mentality, where the values of productive land, clean air, and pure water were of no importance. So some of us went to work and succeeded in making the careless use of our natural resources a real issue, to the point of defeating the government that had been in power for over thirty years.

The Progressive Conservative Party, which succeeded the Social Credit Party, declared the Prime Plan was scrapped and made some very encouraging announcements concerning environmental issues. In due course a very comprehensive policy was drawn up and passed by the legislature, zoning and protecting the east-slope region to control logging and petroleum development. Sewage-treatment regulations were beefed up and environmental concerns in general were given so much better recognition that we sat back and breathed a sigh of relief. But not for long. Whenever people intervene to direct their representatives in government toward more sensible use of their mandate, they should be very aware that winning a battle does not necessarily mean the war is won. There had been two more elections, and the last one, in 1985, gave the government a victory with no opposition.

One day a large brown envelope came in the mail from an anonymous source within government. It contained a blueprint of a much expanded version of the Prime Plan, which involved not only Alberta but Saskatchewan and Manitoba as well. It affected almost every river and watershed from the Peace to the International Border in southern Manitoba. It was unbelievably big. Yet it soon became very apparent that it was—and is—a serious and extremely dangerous plan, a nightmare of expense involving an enormous amount of land. And, of course, part of it was the Three Rivers Dam.

I had never really looked at any dams except in passing. Now that it was important to learn about them, there were two that I wanted to see: the Libby Dam on the Kootenay River just south of the border in Montana, and the Grand Coulee Dam on the Columbia in Washington State. The former was in trouble and had been out of operation almost from the time it was filled. The latter was one of the biggest in the world, and combined electrical-power generation with a massive irrigation project. So I stepped in my car to head west and south to Grand Coulee.

The highway led down below the face of the huge concrete dam to the spick-and-span town of Grand Coulee – a new town that had been built for the people who worked in this big installation. It was a pretty place, with wide streets lined on either side with houses, and adorned with evenly spaced fruit trees all in a mass of bloom. The town was set on a big natural bench below the face of the dam overlooking the river canyon.

About two or three blocks back from the edge of the drop-off above the river, I drove into one end of a wide street to see a curious sight. All along one side, drilling-rigs were busy punching holes in the boulevard between the flowering cherry trees. Then I noticed a crack in the pavement running almost straight up the middle of the street. Parking the car, I walked out to look at it. It appeared to be a fresh crack, a small step about two to three inches high, with the low side toward the river. When I asked a man tending one of the drilling-rigs what was causing it, he gave me a blank look and said he didn't know. A few houses farther along I saw a man in his garden, so I stopped and asked him. He straightened up with a worried frown and said, "We ain't exactly sure, but it looks like this whole place is about to take off and slide into the river." Later he told me: "I'm not supposed to talk about it, so if you want to find out more, you'll have to ask the engineers in charge."

The supervising staff at the dam treated me cordially and invited me to a good lunch, but nothing was forthcoming about the threatened slump on the far side of town. That was a problem they were obviously investigating, and unwilling to discuss. From information received later, I gathered that they apparently were able to stabilize the slump by pumping wet concrete from the surface down onto the bedrock.

I headed back east to Libby, Montana, to find that the dam here is also of concrete, built at the top of a narrow gorge not far from the border. The lake was drawn down, but when full it flooded thousands of acres of prime ranching land north up the valley of the Kootenay for almost fifty miles into Canada. When I visited, a crew was working at the base of the dam with considerable heavy machinery. One of the repair crew summarized the situation neatly: "It ain't no secret. The damn fools that built this thing put it square on an active fault – mostly because it looked like the best place, I guess. Now we're rebuilding the footing under the dam, and it ain't an easy job. We've been busy at it for nearly two years and it ain't finished yet."

Dams can't be built just anywhere on a river, and really top-quality locations are not always available. Building one on a location that looks good but is not grounded on stable rock can be dangerous.

A concrete dam is normally of solid construction, but an earth-filled one has added risks. Consider the case of the Grand Teton Dam in Idaho. This dam had been built against the wishes of the residents of the area, which had been very plainly stated over a number of well-attended public hearings. Among the opponents was a retired geologist, who pointed out that the material to be used for the construction of the dam would not hold water. The bureaucrats and politicians, who (as is too often the case) were basing their proposal for the dam on political, and what turned out to be questionable, economic reasons, totally ignored him and everyone else in opposition, and the dam was built.

One day, when it was about two-thirds full, a tourist stopped on an overlook to take a picture of it. At that moment, squarely in the middle of the dam, water suddenly appeared and began to run down the face. The tourist ran to phone the police, while the breach rapidly widened and the whole structure began to collapse. The valley below the dam was rich farmland dotted with fine homes and buildings, and the area held ten small towns. Fortunately the county sheriff, who knew the geologist, had quietly set up a warning system by phone and now this became a lifeline. The whole valley was vacated with the utmost possible dispatch as the thundering flood bore down on it. Only fourteen people lost their lives. If the break had occurred in the middle of the night, thousands would probably have died. The resulting damages cost the American government a billion dollars. Ironically enough, one of the major purposes of this $85-million project was flood control! It is a historic fact that "flood control" dams tend to increase the severity, while decreasing the frequency, of floods.

As I drove back home, there was plenty to think about, and I was busy mentally outlining and organizing a paper to be presented at the local public hearing. I had come to distrust these events as designed by officials to let people blow off steam, and likely to be ignored if the outcome of the hearing is unfavourable to government plans. But I wanted to give it my best shot.

This particular hearing was well attended, with overwhelming opposition to the Three Rivers Dam project on the Oldman. The fact that no Indians were present surprised me, and I wondered if they were aware of the proposal or had been invited. So I informed the Peigan Band Council of a meeting being held to discuss the dam at a hall in Lundbreck, a few miles down the Crowsnest River from the pass, and they sent a representative to speak for them. He was a powerful and dramatic speaker, well educated and very articulate, who made the government representative sound like a rank amateur on the platform, and he left no doubt of where the tribal council stood in respect to the proposed meddling with the river.

Subsequently the Peigans sent a representation to the Premier's Office in Edmonton, telling him that in reviewing their 1910 agreement for the building of the weir diverting water into the irrigation canal presently in use, they found that they had never been paid for the river bottom on which the weir stood, or the land under the service road attending the canal. In examining the original treaty, they had found that they owned the bottom of the river as well as water rights. They wanted to be paid now – or they would allow no more water to be taken out of the river.

The winter following the hearings wore on, with ominous silence on the part of the government. It was like waiting for a battle that somehow never came off. None of us heard of any decision, and the Peigans received no response to their request. Then came spring, and with the higher water following the break-up, the Peigans sent out a war party. A group of about forty men went down to the flat by the weir, where they camped in tipis and campers. When some irrigation personnel came along to close the weir to begin diverting water into the irrigation canal, they met armed Indians who refused to let them near the weir.

I was working at my desk a few days later with the radio playing in the kitchen when the program was interrupted by a special bulletin. A busload of about forty riot police had just arrived at the weir, plus two patrol cars full of officers; they had been sent by the Attorney General to disperse the Indians. It had to be one of the most callously stupid stunts ever pulled by a government in the entire history of the Royal Canadian Mounted Police. Anyone with an ounce of good sense knows the dangers of a confrontation between armed men over an issue where a case formally stated by the Indians had been ignored by government. All it would take to set off a local war was a shot fired by either side. I listened to the announcement in shock.

Chief Small Legs of the Peigans was at home a few miles from the weir, totally unaware of what was happening until the news bulletin came over the radio. He ran out to his pick-up and roared out of his yard, praying that he wasn't going to be too late. When he arrived, it was to find his men and the police facing each other tensely, their guns much in evidence. Jumping out of his vehicle, he strode purposefully between them, and, holding up a hand, said in a ringing voice, "The first shot fired here goes through my heart!"

Meanwhile a helicopter with the Deputy Minister aboard was circling around overhead, and he was sensible enough to know that he was looking at potential murder and mayhem. At this point in the drama, far from his familiar office desk, he became so sick that the pilot brought the machine down to land not far away. The unfortunate civil servant almost staggered as he walked over to the chief and asked for a drink of water. Towering over the distressed official, the chief waved his hand grandly and intoned, "There's the river! Help yourself!"

Somebody chuckled. That broke the tension, and without another word the police got back in their vehicles and departed, no doubt feeling intensely relieved.

That night the victory drums were beating at the Peigan camp. If some of the old chiefs who signed the Treaty of 1877 were looking back from spirit land at this episode, they must have smiled. Meanwhile, the river flowed serenely through the weir unchecked on its journey to the sea. And very soon the Peigans learned that there is nothing like water, particularly no water, to make men move quickly – even politicians. The Peigans had waited more than half a century for satisfaction in this matter. Shortly after the confrontation, they got paid for their land, and the price was a great deal higher than it would have been in 1910.

Then came a government announcement through the news media that the Three Rivers Dam project had been shelved indefinitely. We wondered how long "indefinitely" might be, for government land-appropriation officials had informed the ranchers due to lose their property that it would be expropriated at a price based on the average price of land in the region. None of the threatened ranchers received notice that the deal was off.

12 *On Dams*

It was time for us to do some studying on the social, economic, and environmental effects of dams, not just here but in the rest of North America and the world. For what was going on in Alberta has been going on all over the globe, particularly in Third World countries, for the past twenty years. From studying collected reports, I found that a picture began to emerge that was revealing and not a little frightening. Because of the limitations of space in a book like this, I will only deal with the aspects of dam-building that are applicable to North America. The issues involved are so numerous, and for the most part so negative, that one has some difficulty knowing where to start. In a world where millions go to bed hungry and very few have access to the clean water and the water-generated power that we in the west take for granted, would it not seem boorish to say that further construction of big dams should be stopped?

Before dams, the major source of water was the tapping of groundwater with wells. In the High Plains country of the United States there are between 150,000 and 200,000 wells being used to supply irrigation systems today. In fact, two-fifths of the water being used for irrigation in the United States in 1980 came from wells. But there is a limit to the number of wells that can be sunk, and it would seem that this has been exceeded all over the world. Indeed, in the American southwest, as a result of over-exploitation, some wells are now spitting out salt water or have gone dry, and irrigation has become so expensive that large areas of agriculture have been taken out of irrigation completely. Unless other water sources are found, the future of farming in the U.S. south-west – which produces twenty per cent of America's food – would seem to be very precarious. In this situation, to many in the afflicted area, Canada's water looks pretty good – no matter what getting it may cost Canadians.

Two other sources of water remain: desalinizing seawater, which is prohibitively expensive, or collecting rainwater, which is too diffuse and unpredictable to be reliable.

So big dams are attractive. They store the water so that it is available when needed and will no longer be wasted on its journey to the sea. Which sounds very good.

But there is another side to this dam-building issue that shows massive ecological destruction, social misery, and impoverishment. It is this side that I want to deal with now.

Big dams are strongly suspected of triggering earthquakes; they have failed to control floods and have actually served to increase flood damage; and they have in many places actually reduced the quality of drinking-water.

It is only recently in our history that we have started building large dams, so our experience has been largely concerned with small ones, which have not proved particularly reliable, for about one per cent of them fail every year. A failure rate of one in a hundred is not considered to be a good gamble in any project analysis, regardless of its ultimate intended use. The failure rate is likely to go up in future; since the good sites are mostly taken up, we can expect to see dams being built in less suitable places, such as the Three Rivers Dam on the Oldman. The failure of the Grand Teton Dam has already been recounted. The Malpasset Dam in France was built in a place of engineering convenience against the advice of consultants. It failed in December 1959, resulting in the death of 491 people. The failure of the Johnstown Dam in New York State in 1889 caused the death of 2,200 people. As I am writing this, news broadcasts are telling of the collapse of a dam at Sargazan in southern Russia owing to torrential rains and mudslides, which has caused the deaths of nineteen people.

It has only recently been recognized that the pressure applied to often fragile geological structures by the vast mass of water impounded by a big dam gives rise to earthquakes.

Lake Mead above Boulder Dam on the Nevada-Arizona border was the first place where seismic activity induced by filling a dam was recorded in the late 1930s. Since then, over an 8,000-square-kilometre area around the lake, 6,000 shocks have been recorded. The Kariba Dam on the Zambezi River in Africa covers an area of 6,649 square kilometres and contains 175 billion cubic metres of water. The filling of the lake started in December 1958 and was completed in 1963. In the first seven months of that year, sixty-three shocks were registered. When the lake was full, a series of particularly strong shocks occurred; ten epicentres were calculated in the deepest part of the lake – one with a magnitude of 6.1 and an after-shock of 6. Before the dam was constructed, this valley was not considered seismic.

Perhaps the Vaiont Dam in Italy provides the most dramatic and tragic example of dam-induced earthquakes. It was filled by September of 1963, and sixty shocks were registered in the first two weeks of that month. Earth began to sluff at the same time along a mountain slope above the lake. It accelerated into a landslide, generating a giant wave that flooded the valley below the dam, wiping out several villages and killing 2,000 people.

The valley of the Oldman here in Alberta is not a likely location for seismic activity. Yet, as Jean Pierre Rothé, who is quoted to some length in *The Social and Environmental Effects of Big Dams*, puts it, "Where he builds dams, man plays the role of sorcerer's appren-

tice: in trying to control the energy of the rivers, he brings about
stresses whose energy can be suddenly and drastically released."

Ironically, the ecological destruction affects not only the dam, but
also, over time, the irrigated land itself. Salinization is the culprit.

Michael Keating in *To the Last Drop* has described salinization as
"an unpleasant side effect in a number of irrigation areas. It is a
process in which excess water lying in the soil dissolves natural salts
in the upper layer of the earth and floats them to the surface. When
the water evaporates, the salt is left behind as a dry, white crust
which sterilizes the land, making it unfit for any crops unless it is
removed."

We all know that the oceans are salt. This salt comes from the
rivers which carry it down from the land, for all soil and rock formations contain salts of various kinds. The clearest mountain stream
will contain up to 50 parts per million of salt, admittedly a mere
fraction of the 35,000 parts per million found in sea water, but
significant just the same. When salt concentration in any soil
reaches 0.5 to 1.0 per cent, the land becomes toxic to plant life.
Ideally, salt in the land should not be closer to the surface than
seven to ten feet. At three to six feet it will cut crop yields to about
half. Closer than that, it wipes out crops entirely.

Irrigation almost inevitably raises the water-table of the land,
particularly if it is overwatered by seepage from canals or too heavy
application. Today, after seventy years of irrigation, there are about
seventy thousand acres on the lower drainages of the Oldman that
are almost useless, or indeed have become useless for growing crops.
This point, of course, has been brought up repeatedly at the hearings. The government agreed to line the main canals to reduce
further leakage and made some vague promises to drain land that
has been salinized.

Careful salt control, to prevent the irrigated land from turning
into a salt-encrusted desert, requires drainage installation, but this
necessity gets no mention in the cost estimates of the Three Rivers

Dam site. At this period of high construction costs of dams, there is just not enough money to cover it. This means that down the line we are looking at heavy losses of good land that at present is being used profitably for livestock range and dryland farming.

Perhaps the most telling ecological argument for engineers who don't care about ecology is what siltation will do to the dam. The whole skin and guts of any water-resource project hinge inevitably on its life expectancy. And that is governed by siltation, which goes hand in hand with environmental destruction. Why should we today pay for a dam disrupting a river system that seriously affects our cultural and historical archaeological sites, fish and wildlife, and agricultural futures, when we know our great-grandchildren will probably curse us bitterly for our short-sightedness in bequeathing them an eyesore full of silt?

We know that sooner or later siltation renders a dam useless. Certainly in Alberta, where the glacial origin of the rivers means that there always has been lots of silt and the abuse of the river-basin forests means that now there is even more, the silt problem is paramount. Long before the proposed dam, diversion, and canal proposals are paid for in produce, the system will be obsolete, silted up to the top, and a real menace to future land use besides, since uses for a giant dam full of silt are not easy to find. When the Diefenbaker Dam on the South Saskatchewan was constructed about forty years ago, we were told that its life expectancy was about one hundred years, which is little enough, but now it is already in a serious condition, and is silting up fast.

A considerable number of American dams are in similar serious difficulty. Most alarming of all, one large dam in China was rendered inoperable by silting up before it was even brought into production.

The real beneficiaries of large-scale dams and water-development schemes are invariably the big multinational companies who build them – and politically well-connected companies like Bechtel spring to mind. The politicians who commissioned the projects in the first place do well by gaining short-term applause for "doing something", and the urban elite do well by taking advantage of real-estate opportunities. We find that the most avid proponents of the Oldman River development are the land speculators who have made large investments in dryland farms based on the plans to bring them under irrigation, thus benefiting from a public subsidy some have valued at $1,000,000 per farm, and some farmers wanting to get out of the business and retire with a pocketful of money.

For those farmers who want to continue farming here, to be uprooted from their homes and lands is a shattering experience. It is all very well to offer people whose lands are being flooded a price equal to the going value of the land in the area. But if they find a piece of suitable replacement land where local values are higher, it is they who have to make up the difference, and those still located on the north side of the lake will have to pay every day for increased transportation costs for hauling goods around the new obstruction of the lake to reach their sources of supply and their market.

It is just plain dishonest for government to blithely tell us that a dam is needed for flood control, when their policy of allowing clear-cutting of timber on the river watershed is a large part of the problem. It is not playing fair to publish a cost accounting that does not include the damages to fish and wildlife, or the loss of the valuable produce of the land being flooded and the taxes it has generated. It is not reasonable to leave out the value of the annual crops presently being raised on the dryland areas scheduled to be irrigated. Above all, it is heartless not to include the social impact of forcing people out of their homes in the cost accounting.

The total land suitable for agriculture in Canada is seven per cent of the country as a whole. We cannot afford to repeat the process they have gone through to their sorrow in the United States, where land speculation and the lobbying pressure on government by big industry which builds dams have been the underlying force behind water-resource development. Short-term projects have an inevitable way of turning into long-term losses. Canada does not have enough good land to play around with water-resource development schemes that will wipe out uncounted acres. Nor can this country afford to drown valuable forests, as has been done under the Mica Creek Dam in British Columbia, and the Bennett Lake on the Peace River project, where the rotting trees in the dam have made the "recreation centre" promises ring hollow.

Anyone who has enjoyed the deeply moving sight of the huge salmon runs on the Fraser and its tributaries can appreciate the enormous value of this food source to the country. I have seen spring salmon weighing up to sixty and seventy pounds spawning below the falls not far downriver from Yellowhead Pass; fish that have come well over a thousand miles in their dramatic migration from the Pacific. The same values apply to the magnificent Skeena River system and the Stikine. To trade this for the questionable profits of selling electricity to the industrial, heavily populated areas of Washington, Oregon, and California does not make sense.

Fish are a valuable source of food as long as water continues to run unimpeded down these valleys, and the tourist income from the sport fishery is also important. The Oldman River is valuable as a tourist attraction, an aspect that has never been given any importance by the promoters of dams anywhere. It is a well-known fact that the ecological impact of cutting a river off by building a dam is so dramatic that it results in the loss of the fishery. A river ecosystem is continuous from its head to its delta on the coast. A dam cuts it into segments, which kills out the natural fish population. The Columbia used to host the biggest salmon runs in the world. After damming, the fishery is almost gone, despite the expenditure of millions of dollars to try to preserve it.

The politicians and bureaucrats generally boast about the formation of such a new dam's lake for its added recreational values. It is a carrot that tempts very few, particularly where the future of the Three Rivers Dam site is concerned; for the location is directly downwind from the Crowsnest Pass, probably Alberta's greatest natural wind tunnel. Winds can reach velocities up to and beyond a hundred miles an hour on short notice in the valleys of the Oldman, and it is not wise to be caught out in any kind of boat under these conditions. How anyone could get a boat to the water during periods of low draw-down in late summer and fall is a question the government does not address, among many other important ones.

Do large dams live up to the promises of engineers who design them and oversee their building? According to case studies, the answer is often no.

Too often hydraulic engineers have little knowledge of hydrology, watershed management, and river fluctuations, and just as often have no sympathy for or understanding of environmental, social, or economic analysis. Most of them have absolutely no training in ecological impacts. Yet these same engineers are given the tremendous responsibility of applying their expertise on detailed things like embankment and spillway design to the resource management of entire river basins. No wonder people, fish and wildlife, and cultural and agricultural interests end up holding the short end of a very slippery stick.

It would seem to be vitally important that if we are to survive, we must develop and adopt holistic engineering techniques where the spirits of our rivers are recognized. Where the Oldman is concerned, its spiritual connotations were recognized by those who came before us for thousands of years. What is to prevent us from renewing that relationship? The sure knowledge that the whole projection of a very complicated and astronomically expensive water-resource scheme here in Alberta will end up with silt-choked rivers from one end of the province to the other long before it is paid for is a good reason to sit back and give the whole problem a long and understanding look.

We owe it to those who follow us. Just because the United States followed a blind trail in that country's development of water resources for the wrong reasons and now finds itself facing deep trouble is no reason for us to do the same. At this moment the federal government in Washington will not issue a permit to build any dam unless the builders applying for it can prove that the people most affected by it also want it and why. They have learned that following blindly behind pork-barrel politicians – and big water projects are the most expensive cuts of pork – and greedy engineering companies, always happy to make campaign contributions, can be very expensive and too often very final.

Still, appallingly extensive – and expensive – proposals are being promoted. The North American Water and Power Alliance being proposed by the Ralph M. Parsons Company of Pasadena, California, among others, would divert water from Alaska and northern Canada to various parts of Canada, the United States, and Mexico. Various hydro-electric plants scattered along it would generate a capacity of 70,000 megawatts – the equal of about seventy nuclear-power plants – apart from the water it would pump. The drainage area affected would be about 1.3 million square miles and 160 million acre feet of water would be diverted south. The estimated costs would be in the neighbourhood of $200 billion, but if experience is anything to go by, this could be three to four times higher.

In the southwestern United States, the massive demand for water and the mindless political manoeuvring to get it have resulted in a precipitous fall of groundwater reserves, in rivers running dry, and in widespread salt-poisoning of the land. It has reached a position there where human demands are fast exceeding the natural life-support sytems. We must ask ourselves why we should fall into this trap here in Canada, particularly in Alberta's Oldman River basin, where we still have time to take a more careful look.

Whether the opportunity will be taken is another question, for the government announced in 1984 that recess was over for the people due to be drowned out by the Three Rivers Dam project – "indefinite" had again become the definite. And somewhere along the line the name had been changed. In Michael Keating's words:

"One provincial official said that he suspected the name of the project was changed from the old title of Three Rivers Dam to Old-man Dam 'so it would only look like we were messing up one river instead of three.'"

The government ordered another program of impact studies, as though the environmental and cultural effects would be different after a short period of inactivity. The only thing that had changed was the estimates of costs, which had gone up – $550 million now, but which will, by my estimates, likely be closer to $1 billion.

Again, a whole series of public hearings was held after notices had been mailed to all interested people, and as usual the majority were in opposition. Just as most of us predicted, no attention has been paid to our objections. The reports resulting from the various studies that have been done have never been published, which would seem to indicate that they must not have been suitably positive about the benefits of the dam.

To the white men and the Peigans, whose reservation and lands flank both sides of the river for miles, everything the Oldman represents and has nourished for ten thousand years is in jeopardy. If future generations are to be inheritors and not just survivors, we have an obligation to act with firmness and utter finality in its protection. There is no legacy in all nature to compare to a free-flowing river. The Peigans know this, and again they are taking action by launching lawsuits against both the provincial and the federal governments to protect their water rights and their land. Back in the old days it was often the Indians who blazed the trails we followed later. Maybe today their descendants will again show us the way to live with their holy river.

13 *The End of the Trail?*

We have followed the old-time people on a long trail, where the only signs have been their stone weapons and tools, some scarred bones showing butchering marks, their carved ivory and bone tools, their campfire ashes, and, in a few places, their skeletal remains. It has led us through a vast expanse of mountains, hills, and plains from the northern rim of the continent south through the old corridor between the two major ice masses to the open country and beyond, then back again to the birthing valley of the Oldman River – the holy river of the Blackfoot people. The trail has taken us through a great, lonely land across some terrifying places as well as locations so utterly beautiful and awe-inspiring that they eternally call to the souls of all who pass that way.

We have looked at a slow-moving drama of human history, where nature was carving mountain slopes and valleys, shaping the contours that we see today. We have watched the kaleidoscope of shifting actions, the development of human cultures along with the animals on which they preyed and with which they co-existed as a part of nature and not its enemy. They lived under the same big sky showing blue in the sun of a clear day and turning deep purple at night, under a canopy of shining stars. They survived storms, hunger, floods, the extremes of hot and cold, and a myriad of dangers with only their skin clothing and shelters to keep them warm and their primitive weapons and tools to sustain them through the seasons. The winters were savage, but they watched the clouds running like pony tails streaming in the winds of spring and summer and prayed to the sun – knowing that from it all life sprang.

I have attempted to guide you on this life story of a river – drawing pictures with words of a country that has changed in my short life, and is no longer so pristine and lovely as when I first saw it. I have tried to show you the river in its true living light; the way it has influenced the cultures of the people who have lived along it for countless generations caught in its spell. I have endeavoured to illustrate why the old native cultures survived for so many thousands of years, living happily and successfully until they met another dominating culture in our time, when, for a while, they have had much difficulty in adjusting to it.

For when the Europeans intruded into this great island between the Atlantic and Pacific oceans, the peoples who lived here became victims, like all the native cultures of the world, of insidious, unrelenting plundering, which has known no satisfying of its greed. Here, first, it was the fur trade in which the Indians were used to gather pelts to trade for things they quickly came to think they needed. It was not long before beavers and other fur-bearers became very scarce. The buffalo, the staple support of the Plains people, were wiped out in a mindless slaughter for their robes. Then came the following flood of land-hungry white settlers who have been mindlessly plundering it ever since, mincing up the very soil until it blows away, and devastating the forests so that good timber will not grow again for centuries.

We have not been very far-sighted or even consistent in putting dollar signs on every resource we wish to plunder since we came to this country. But we have overlooked putting any value on those resources we destroy and waste in the course of our plundering. We have not been balancing the natural books.

Where, for instance, is the advantage of building a dam on the

Oldman River when we take thousands of acres of valuable agricultural land out of production to irrigate thousands more acres presently in viable dryland farming downstream? Where is the profit in destroying a sport fishery of untold value to the tourist industry, along with the wintering range of a thousand deer, by actual count, to say nothing of countless small birds and animals that will lose their habitat in the three valleys that will be flooded? Where is the advantage of conducting expensive surveys of the social, fish and wildlife, and historic archaeological impacts of this project and then refusing to publish them so that the people, who are paying for it, will not have the chance to know what they are losing? Why clear-cut the timber on the headwaters of the river, with a heavy public subsidy of the roads to reach the areas involved, then use the excuse of flood control for justifying the building of the dam, at the same time ignoring the accelerated siltation that will much more rapidly put it out of production? Where is the intelligence involved in government promotion extolling the economic advantages of more irrigation when we know that the only people who will benefit financially – for a short time – are the politicians, engineering contractors, and land speculators?

No amount of political window-dressing can hide the real answers to these questions or the fact that the economic books can never be balanced where the people being displaced, the ecological damages, and all of us who are paying the cost are concerned. If there were not so many examples of the absolute folly of such developments all over the world for reference, it might be more understandable. But there are many fully documented precedents to prove that we cannot afford to build such a construction or even start to pay for the ecological, environmental, and economic damages that will result. We will continue to fight against this cold-blooded, premeditated act of government folly, to preserve the river we love.

Meanwhile, the Oldman still flows unshackled across the prairie toward the sea. The spirit of the river is not dead.

Epilogue

The fight to save the Oldman River was prolonged and bitter. There were lawsuits and hearings, and even though we won most of them in court, the provincial government was adamantly stubborn about the issue and went ahead with their plans to build the dam in spite of the court decisions. The excuse they gave was the pressing need for agricultural irrigation. But this was deliberately misleading, for the government's refusal to drop the plan had nothing to do with agriculture; it was industrial. The province had been building roads like crazy, the contractors had been buying more and more machines and the government had been lending them the money to do it. But even in a big province like Alberta, road building has its limitations, and now the contractors were clamouring for more work, so they could pay their debts. To help them, the government had come up with grandiose well-publicized construction schemes like the Oldman River Dam.

As this book explains, the Friends of the Oldman, our organization, had some very definite misgivings about the dam. We knew that the runoff from the mountains would soon fill it up with silt. And we knew the dangers of the location below the junction of the river's three forks (Castle River, Crowsnest River and the North Fork) because we had seen what happens when warm June rains come down on a heavy blanket of winter snow, and all three forks run wild. Any earth-filled dam is a goner if the water in the reservoir ever tops it and flushes out its earth core. If that were to happen with the Oldman River Dam the resulting destruction would be horrendous. Our calculations showed that in the river channel below the dam the standing wave would be thirty to forty feet high and it would be travelling close to forty kilometres per hour. It would hit the Peigan Indian Reserve like a tidal wave in thirty to forty minutes. The loss of life and property down river could be catastrophic.

Our association was headed by a remarkable woman, Martha Kostuch, and she never let up in her determination to save the river. Over the years of our fight she had accumulated an impressive file, which she took to Ottawa and presented to the Supreme Court of Canada. After careful consideration of her evidence, the Supreme Court ordered the Federal Government to set up a Commission to go out to Alberta and conduct an environmental study of the entire issue, including interviews with the people whose land had been expropriated. This took some time, but in due course the Commission's report was tendered to the Federal Government. It found that the location and construction of the dam was faulty, and recommended that it be destroyed.

The Provincial Government of Alberta and the Federal Government of Canada, who shared the power in the matter, did nothing about it.

Consequently, the Oldman River Dam, completed in 1991, even though it ran way over budget in an attempt to make it safe, seems to me like an accident waiting to happen. In the spring of 1995 there was a flood which came very close to going over the dam. Another foot or two and it would have flowed over the top, likely washing out the earth at its core, then sweeping away the hollow shell. But with downstream disaster on the cards, the weather changed just in time to save the dam.

But the damage has already been done. The Peigan Indians have now evacuated their beautiful valley. Many of the women are afraid to go into it to pick berries in August, as they have done for generations.

Sadly, the damming of the historic Oldman is a prime example of politicians failing to follow their own laws, because dollars have been deemed more important than people. We have lots of law in Canada, but we sometimes run very short of justice.

Andy Russell
February 2000

Acknowledgements

In writing this book, I have been helped immensely by the previous works of many people. My research has covered more material than can possibly be mentioned here, since it involves hundreds of papers and books. One truly fascinating source of information is *The Palaeoecology of the Beringia*, edited by David M. Hopkins, John V. Mathews, Jr., Charles E. Schweyer, and Steven B. Young; published by Academic Press, New York. The focus of this volume is a collection of studies focusing on the unglaciated Arctic during the last Ice Age, indicating that from 45,000 to 11,000 years B.P. (before the present), an environment considerably more productive and diverse than the present one existed. For those readers wishing to delve more seriously into the prehistory of North America, this book is a rewarding experience.

The prologue, in which I reconstructed a hunt by applying my personal knowledge and experience of the motivations and needs of men who live by their ability to cope with the animals available to them for food and shelter, is intended to give the reader a glimpse of what life was like back there in those early times. I hope that it and the succeeding chapters on Indian life will perhaps serve to highlight a portion of our history that has been largely overlooked. We have been prone to think that the North American story began when Europeans arrived on this continent, when in truth some very dynamic cultures preceded them by many thousands of years. It is my belief that only by recognizing and studying these cultures can we truly come to know our own. For these peoples survived, travelled, and flourished without plundering and wasting the resources supporting them; some of them have even survived the severe transitions that we imposed on them. Surely we have the wits and wisdom to profit by their experience, for looking back, with some understanding and recognition, helps us to look ahead and avoid the dangers confronting us. Pir Nilyat Khan has said: "Sometimes one's search leads one back into the distant past to rediscover our legacy, the testimony of lives, of visions, of experiences – signatures on the surfaces of the earth."

Looking at the Libby Dam and the Grand Coulee Dam led me to find out about others across the world, most of them built within the last twenty years, with the resulting discovery that almost all of them are dealing with dangerous problems threatening humans, land, fish, and wildlife. The Indians will not be surprised when I say that we have been exploiting what seems obvious to us in our drive for hydro power, building dams and atomic plants, destroying our rivers, and threatening ourselves with lethal pollution, and all the while we have completely overlooked the greatest natural power source in our universe: the sun and the wind. We talk of cheap irrigation and electrical power, generated by dams; yet if we think of the future losses in drowned land, human displacement, disease, salinization of the land, and the many other resource losses involved, it is perhaps the most expensive method ever devised.

In 1984 a report to the European Ecological Action Group in Bordeaux, France, by Nicholas Hildyard and Edward Goldsmith was published by the Wadebridge Ecological Centre, Worthyville Manor, Camelford, Cornwall, PL32 9TT, U.K. The first two volumes, totalling 677 pages, consist of a comprehensive collection of studies of the large dams of the world. The third will be available in August 1987. This clearly written and revealing document covers all the major dams of the world and deals with every aspect of them. It is absolutely required reading for anyone interested in dams, especially those who have been told how many advantages will be forthcoming from their construction for power and irrigation.

Another book, *To the Last Drop*, by Michael Keating, published by Macmillan of Canada, is highly recommended.

My chapters on the prehistoric Indians' ways of life have been gathered across the years from so many sources, including the Indians themselves, that I can mention very few. John Snow's very revealing book *These Mountains Are Our Sacred Places*, published by Samuel Stevens of Toronto, was a valuable source of information on the Stoney Indians. My thanks also go to Hugh Dempsey of the Glenbow Museum for his help, and for the information from his excellent books, which I warmly recommend. *The Fur Trade in Canada*, by Harold A. Innis, published by the University of Toronto Press, and *Native Peoples: The Canadian Experience*, by R. Bruce Morrison and C. Roderick Wilson, published by McClelland and Stewart of Toronto, are also excellent sources.

My warm thanks, too, go to Tim Losey for his unswerving help throughout what has been a fascinating, though sometimes difficult, journey for me in my efforts to illuminate a picture of our past history and our present dilemma.

I can only hope that the result is sufficiently revealing, and, along with many others, pray that the Oldman River will continue to flow wild and free. At the very least, this book will serve to show those who follow us, and who will be charged with the task of correcting the mistakes of their forebears, that some of us cared, and really tried to make them inheritors of a natural wonder and not just survivors of the brutish greed and ignorance of those who thought they could improve on nature.

Andy Russell

Andy Russell, born in 1915, grew up on a ranch in the Foothills of the Rocky Mountains. He left high school in Lethbridge to head out to the Rockies as a trapper, then worked as a cowboy and ranch hand before becoming a trail guide. After thirty years of this, he began to photograph the wildlife around him, and to write about it. Soon he was a famous and bestselling author, with books such as *Grizzly Country*, *Horns in the High Country*, *The High West*, *The Rockies*, *Memoirs of a Mountain Man*, *The Life of a River*, *The Canadian Cowboy*, and *Andy Russell's Campfire Stories*. A member of the Order of Canada, the recipient of three honorary degrees, and an elected member of the Explorers Club, Andy Russell lives on a ranch bordering Waterton Lakes National Park, Alberta.

More from Andy Russell . . .

The Canadian Cowboy

BY ANDY RUSSELL

ILLUSTRATED BY DON BRESTLER

**As one old-timer remarked, it's pretty hard to kill a cowboy:
"About the only way to be sure is to cut off his head and hide
it someplace where he can't find it."**

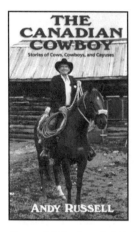

This is the history of a rare and tough breed, the Canadian cowboy. Concentrating on Alberta, but with a tip of the ten-gallon hat to the ranching country in Saskatchewan and British Columbia, the author pays tribute to the hardy pioneers who founded the ranching way of life in Mexico, then brought it north through Texas and across the plains to Canada.

Who better to tell the story of the Canadian cowboy than former bronco-buster and mountain man Andy Russell? Enlivened by personal anecdote, and beautifully illustrated throughout by western artist Don Brestler, *The Canadian Cowboy* hit the *Globe and Mail* bestseller list when it was first published, and delighted readers and reviewers alike:

"*The Canadian Cowboy* is a long conversation with . . . a man whose memories of life
in the rural west are studded with lore and wisdom, tall tales and gentle humour.
City slickers might feel they're intruding around Russell's campfire but he
soon puts us all at our ease." – *Toronto Life*

"It's not possible to do justice to any of his stories just by outlining what they are about.
You have to . . . imagine hearing the booming voice of this giant of a man, and start
reading. You won't want the night to end." – *Saskatoon Star-Phoenix*

ISBN 0-7710-7881-1   Trade paperback   288 pages   6" x 9"

Andy Russell's Campfire Stories

BY ANDY RUSSELL

ILLUSTRATED BY DON BRESTLER

The favourite stories of Canada's most celebrated cowboy and Rocky Mountain raconteur

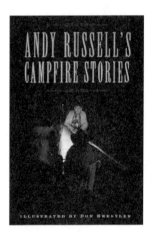

As the dark closes in and the fire settles down to a deep and warming glow, there's no nightcap better than a good story well told. Andy Russell is a master storyteller, and this collection of new and previously published tales evokes as if by magic the irresistible allure of the campfire. It's not hard to imagine the starry sky above and the gentle sounds of the pack horses nearby.

Some of Andy's tales are about his own youth; others are part of the western lore and the history of the west. Some are about wild horses, grizzlies, or bighorn sheep; or they may concern those whose trails crossed his, or whose legends he heard over campfires long ago.

What all these yarns have in common is the unique style of the best-known of all Canadian cowboys, the inimitable Andy Russell.

"Another dandy collection featuring 38 tales of wildlife, trappers, cowboys, anglers, mountain men, frontier women, Native history, Hollywood excess and beyond, beautifully illustrated by the Charlie Russell-esque line drawings of his friend down the road, Don Brestler." – *Edmonton Journal*

"Russell is the tops. . . . There is so much to learn while having a good time with a master story-teller." – *Saskatoon Star-Phoenix*

ISBN 0-7710-7884-6   Trade paperback   328 pages   6" x 9"

PUBLISHED BY McCLELLAND & STEWART INC.

W.O. MITCHELL COUNTRY: Portrayed *by* Courtney Milne, Text *by* W.O. Mitchell
W.O.'s writings about the Prairies, the Foothills and the Mountains, selected by Orm and Barbara Mitchell, have inspired Courtney Milne to produce matching full-colour photographs. A feast for the eye and the mind.
Art/Photography, 10½ × 11½, 240 pages, 200 colour photographs, hardcover

WHO HAS SEEN THE WIND *by* W.O. Mitchell *illustrated by* William Kurelek
W. O. Mitchell's best-loved book, this Canadian classic of childhood on the prairies is presented in its full, unexpurgated edition, and is "gorgeously illustrated." *Calgary Herald*
Fiction, 8½ × 10, 320 pages, numerous colour and black-and-white illustrations, trade paperback

TEN LOST YEARS: Memories of Canadians Who Survived the Depression *by* Barry Broadfoot
Filled with unforgettable true stories, this uplifting classic of oral history, first published in 1973, is "a moving chronicle of human tragedy and moral triumph during the hardest of times." *Time*
Non-fiction, 5⅞ × 9, 442 pages, 24 pages of photographs, trade paperback

RED BLOOD: One (Mostly) White Guy's Encounter With the Native World *by* Robert Hunter
The founder of Greenpeace looks back on a wild, hell-raising career. "Hunter acts. He does things. . . . In all his adventures humour is a companion, but he can also write angry political commentary." *Globe and Mail*
Non-fiction, 6 × 9, 280 pages, hardcover

CONFESSIONS OF AN IGLOO DWELLER *by* James Houston
The famous novelist and superb storyteller who brought Inuit art to the outside world recounts his Arctic adventures between 1948 and 1962. "Sheer entertainment, as fascinating as it is charming." *Kirkus Reviews*
Memoir/Travel, 6 × 9, 320 pages, maps, drawings, trade paperback

ZIGZAG: A Life on the Move *by* James Houston
This "remarkable account" (*Books in Canada*) ranges from the Arctic to New York and beyond and tells of Presidents, hunters, glass factory gaffers, leopards, walrus, movies, bestselling books and 10,000-year-old meatballs.
Memoir/Travel, 6 × 9, 288 pages, drawings, trade paperback

NEXT-YEAR COUNTRY: Voices of Prairie People *by* Barry Broadfoot
"There's something mesmerizing about these authentic Canadian voices."
Globe and Mail "A good book, a joy to read." *Books in Canada*
Oral history, 5⅜ × 8¾, 400 pages, trade paperback

WELCOME TO FLANDERS FIELDS: The First Canadian Battle of the
Great War – Ypres, 1915 *by* Daniel G. Dancocks
"A magnificent chronicle of a terrible battle . . . Daniel Dancocks is spell-
binding throughout." *Globe and Mail*
Military/History, 4¼ × 7, 304 pages, photos, maps, paperback

ACROSS THE BRIDGE: Stories *by* Mavis Gallant
These eleven stories, set mostly in Montreal or in Paris, were described as
"Vintage Gallant – urbane, witty, absorbing." *Winnipeg Free Press* "We
come away from it both thoughtful and enriched." *Globe and Mail*
Fiction, 6 × 9, 208 pages, trade paperback

AT THE COTTAGE: A Fearless Look at Canada's Summer Obsession *by*
Charles Gordon *illustrated by* Graham Pilsworth
This perennial best-selling book of gentle humour is "a delightful re-
minder of why none of us addicted to cottage life will ever give it up."
Hamilton
Spectator　　　*Humour, 6 × 9, 224 pages, illustrations, trade paperback*

A PASSION FOR NARRATIVE: A Guide for Writing Fiction *by* Jack
Hodgins
"One excellent path from original to marketable manuscript. . . . It would
take a beginning writer years to work her way through all the goodies
Hodgins offers." *Globe and Mail*
Non-fiction/Writing guide, 5¼ × 8½, 216 pages, trade paperback

OVER FORTY IN BROKEN HILL: Unusual Encounters in the Australian
Outback *by* Jack Hodgins
"Australia described with wit, wonder and affection by a bemused visitor
with Canadian sensibilities." *Canadian Press* "Damned fine writing." *Books
in Canada*　　　*Travel, 5½ × 8½, 216 pages, trade paperback*

DANCING ON THE SHORE: A Celebration of Life at Annapolis Basin *by*
Harold Horwood, *Foreword by* Farley Mowat
"A Canadian *Walden*" *Windsor Star* that "will reward, provoke, challenge
and enchant its readers." *Books in Canada*
Nature/Ecology, 5⅛ × 8¼, 224 pages, 16 wood engravings, trade paperback

HUGH MACLENNAN'S BEST: An anthology *selected by* Douglas Gibson
This selection from all of the works of the witty essayist and famous novelist is "wonderful . . . It's refreshing to discover again MacLennan's formative
influence on our national character." *Edmonton Journal*
Anthology, 6 × 9, 352 pages, trade paperback

ACCORDING TO JAKE AND THE KID: A Collection of New Stories *by*
W.O. Mitchell
"This one's classic Mitchell. Humorous, gentle, wistful, it's 16 new short
stories about life through the eyes of Jake, a farmhand, and the kid, whose
mom owns the farm." *Saskatoon Star-Phoenix*
Fiction, 5 × 7¾, 280 pages, trade paperback

THE BLACK BONSPIEL OF WILLIE MACCRIMMON *by* W.O. Mitchell
illustrated by Wesley W. Bates
A devil of a good tale about curling – W.O.Mitchell's most successful comic
play now appears as a story, fully illustrated, for the first time, and it is "a
true Canadian classic." *Western Report*
Fiction, 4⅝ × 7½, 144 pages with 10 wood engravings, hardcover

FOR ART'S SAKE: A new novel *by* W.O. Mitchell
"*For Art's Sake* shows the familiar Mitchell brand of subtle humour in this
tale of an aging artist who takes matters into his own hands in bringing
pictures to the people." *Calgary Sun*   *Fiction, 6 × 9, 240 pages, hardcover*

LADYBUG, LADYBUG . . . by W.O. Mitchell
"Mitchell slowly and subtly threads together the elements of this richly de-
tailed and wonderful tale . . . the outcome is spectacular . . . *Ladybug,
Ladybug* is certainly among the great ones!" *Windsor Star*
Fiction, 4¼ × 7, 288 pages, paperback

ROSES ARE DIFFICULT HERE *by* W.O.Mitchell
"Mitchell's newest novel is a classic, capturing the richness of the small
town, and delving into moments that really count in the lives of its
people . . ." *Windsor Star*   *Fiction, 6 × 9, 328 pages, trade paperback*

THE ASTOUNDING LONG-LOST LETTERS OF DICKENS OF THE
MOUNTED *edited by* Eric Nicol
The "letters"from Charles Dickens's son, a Mountie from 1874 to 1886, are
"a glorious hoax . . . so cleverly crafted, so subtly hilarious." *Vancouver Sun*
Fiction, 4¼ × 7, 296 pages, paperback

PADDLE TO THE AMAZON: The Ultimate 12,000-Mile Canoe Adventure *by* Don Starkell *edited by* Charles Wilkins
From Winnipeg to the mouth of the Amazon by canoe! "This real-life adventure book . . . must be ranked among the classics of the literature of survival." *Montreal Gazette* "Fantastic." Bill Mason
Adventure, 6 × 9, 320 pages, maps, photos, trade paperback

THE HONORARY PATRON: A novel *by* Jack Hodgins
The Governor General's Award-winner's thoughtful and satisfying third novel of a celebrity's return home to Vancouver Island mixes comedy and wisdom "and it's magic." *Ottawa Citizen*
Fiction, 4¼ × 7, 336 pages, paperback

INNOCENT CITIES: A novel *by* Jack Hodgins
Victorian in time and place, this delightful new novel by the author of *The Invention of the World* proves once again that "as a writer, Hodgins is unique among his Canadian contemporaries." *Globe and Mail*
Fiction, 4¼ × 7, 416 pages, paperback

THE CUNNING MAN: A novel *by* Robertson Davies
This "sparkling history of the erudite and amusing Dr. Hullah who knows the souls of his patients as well as he knows their bodies" *London Free Press* is "wise, humane and constantly entertaining." *The New York Times*
Fiction, 6 × 9, 480 pages, hardcover

PADDLE TO THE ARCTIC *by* Don Starkell
The author of *Paddle to the Amazon* "has produced another remarkable book" *Quill & Quire*. His 5,000-kilometre trek across the Arctic by kayak or dragging a sled is a "fabulous adventure story." *Halifax Daily News*
Adventure, 6 × 9, 320 pages, maps, photos, trade paperback

THE MACKEN CHARM: A novel *by* Jack Hodgins
When the rowdy Mackens gather for a family funeral on Vancouver Island in the 1950s, the result is "fine, funny, sad and readable, a great yarn, the kind only an expert storyteller can produce." *Ottawa Citizen*
Fiction, 6 × 9, 320 pages, trade paperback

SELECTED STORIES *by* Alice Munro
"The collection of the year," said *Kirkus Reviews* of these 28 superb stories representing Alice Munro's best. "The whole volume makes one believe anew in fiction's power to transfigure." *Washington Post*
Fiction, 6¼ × 9¼, 560 pages, hardcover

THE MERRY HEART: Selections 1980-1995 *by* Robertson Davies
"A marvellous array of Davies' speeches and reviews, interspersed with bits of his personal diaries." *Hamilton Spectator* "It's a happy thing that the voice from the attic is still being heard." *Montreal Gazette*
                                    Non-fiction, 6 × 9, 400 pages, hardcover

THE SELECTED STORIES OF MAVIS GALLANT *by* Mavis Gallant
"A volume to hold and to treasure" said the *Globe and Mail* of the 52 marvellous stories selected from Mavis Gallant's life's work. "It should be in every reader's library."   *Fiction, 6⅛ × 9¼ , 900 pages, trade paperback*

HITLER VERSUS ME: The Return of Bartholomew Bandy *by* Donald Jack
Bandy ("a national treasure" according to a Saskatoon reviewer) is back in the RCAF, fighting Nazis and superior officers, and trying to keep his age and his toupee as secret as the plans for D-Day.
                                    Fiction/Humour, 6 × 9 , 360 pages, hardcover

THE CANADA TRIP *by* Charles Gordon
Charles Gordon and his wife drove from Ottawa to St. John's to Victoria and back. The result is "a very human, warm, funny book" (*Victoria Times Colonist*) that will set you planning your own trip.
                                    Travel/Humour, 6 × 9, 364 pages, 22 maps, trade paperback

THE ICE MASTER: A Novel of the Arctic *by* James Houston
Part sea-story (involving a mutiny and a hurricane), part Arctic saga that tells of Inuit and Yankee whalers in the North in 1876, this rousing historical novel is "a straight-away adventure." *Winnipeg Free Press*
                                    Fiction, 6 × 9, 368 pages, 40 drawings, trade paperback

AN EVENING WITH W.O. MITCHELL *by* W.O. Mitchell
"A collection of 31 of Mitchell's favourite stories . . . which he regularly performed with ebullience and dramatic flair to delighted audiences across the country." *Toronto Star* "An excellent performance." *Saskatoon StarPhoenix*
                                    Anthology, 6 × 9, 320 pages, 30 photographs, trade paperback

HAPPY ALCHEMY: Writings on the Theatre and Other Lively Arts *by* Robertson Davies
"Far more personal than anything published under Davies's name, and all the more enjoyable for it" (*Edmonton Sun*), this collection shows the full range of his wit and wisdom.   *Non-fiction, 6 × 9, 400 pages, hardcover*

THE LOVE OF A GOOD WOMAN: Stories *by* Alice Munro
"Her stories *feel* like novels," writes Robert MacNeil. The power of love –
and of sex – is the theme of these eight marvellous new stories by the
writer who has been described by the *Washington Post* as "our Chekhov."
Fiction, 6 × 9, 352 pages, hardcover

BROKEN GROUND: A novel *by* Jack Hodgins
It's 1922 and the shadow of the First World War hangs over a struggling
Soldier's Settlement on Vancouver Island. This powerful novel with its
flashbacks to the trenches is "a richly, deeply human book – a joy to read."
W.J. Keith   *Fiction, 6 × 9, 368 pages, trade paperback*

FOR YOUR EYE ALONE: Letters 1976-1995 *by* Robertson Davies
These lively letters, selected and edited by Judith Skelton Grant, give an
"over the shoulder" look at the private Davies, at the height of his international fame, writing family notes and slicing up misguided reviewers.
Belles lettres, 6 × 9, 400 pages, facsimile letters, notes, index, hardcover

HIDEAWAY: Life on the Queen Charlotte Islands *by* James Houston
After a life of igloo dwelling and zigzagging James Houston found the
perfect Pacific hideaway. With its tales of the Haida and their legends, and
of eagles, salmon and the rainforest, this is a tribute to a magic place.
Memoir/Travel, 6 × 9, 272 pages, map, 65 illustrations, hardcover

HOW I SPENT MY SUMMER HOLIDAYS *by* W.O.Mitchell
A novel that rivals *Who has seen the Wind*. "Astonishing . . . Mitchell
turns the pastoral myth of prairie boyhood inside out." *Toronto Star*
Fiction, 5½ × 8½, 276 pages, trade paperback